THE
Power
OF
Connection
IN THE
Church

A Church Leader's Guide for Connecting
Guests and Closing the Back Door

STEVE CHESNUT

To my love, Gabrielle, and our amazing
children, Steven, Karis, and Ava

To Pastor Jeff & Brandy, for connecting to us,
pastoring us, and inviting us to use our gifts in the church

To the Milestone staff team, and our Milestone family,
for relentlessly loving people with intentionality,
authenticity, and sincerity

CONTENTS

SECTION III

THE PROCESS OF CONNECTION   135

FOREWORD

Stop for a moment and think about this:

The uncreated, eternal God, the creator of the universe—the perfect and loving Father who knew you before you were born and uniquely fashioned you with special gifts and abilities—has a place for you on His team.

If that was not enough, He also tells you He loves you, not on your best day, but at your lowest moment.

He wants a relationship with you before you can ever do anything for Him or be of any special use to Him.

He does not need you. And yet, He wants you.

Because of His grace and mercy, He offers forgiveness for your sins, hope for your brokenness, health for your dysfunction, and joy for your pain.

He invites you into the mysterious and boundless peace only available when we offer this same grace and mercy to others.

He has this dream to build a family—a place where people of every ethnicity from every background on the planet come together in His Son to be His special people in the earth.

He lovingly extends this invitation to anyone who would receive Him.

Now tell me, no matter what tradition someone comes from, no matter how much pain they have experienced in their past, no matter how busy their life is—*who would say no to this?*

When many people hear the word "church," they don't think of what I've just described to you. But it is the picture God paints in His Word.

As church leaders, our challenge is to help the people experience this—not to hear someone else talk about it, but to see it for themselves.

The problem is not with God and His Church; the issue is with our inability to connect people to the vision.

Any church that finds a way to connect people to this message will grow.

We all want to be part of something special. I have found most people are not afraid of hard work when they understand the significance of their contribution and the value of the goal.

I believe there are no goals more valuable than building a healthy church. Because you are reading this book, I have a feeling you agree.

Leaders want the church to grow. We want to use our gifts to serve people so that as many people as possible have the opportunity to enter into a genuine relationship with God. This gets us out of bed in the morning. It is a calling worthy of our whole lives.

Unfortunately, there's a disconnect between what we think we are communicating and what the people are actually experiencing. It is so easy to get so caught up in our projects and initiatives that we lose sight of what it feels like from their perspective.

We can get so caught up in *our* world that we lose sight of *theirs*.

I've been a long-time student of church and how it works. There's nothing I love more than to talk about it with people who love it too and discuss ways to make it better. I love every part of what we do in ministry. But I also realize there are many things we do that do not translate to the everyday life of the people we are trying to reach.

The problem is not a lack of effort. The problem is, we are focused on the wrong things.

This is the purpose of connection. More than a department on the team, too often connection is the missing ingredient of the recipe. More than the responsibility of a few individuals, it must be on the mind of the whole team—from the senior leader to the newest volunteer.

We have all been exposed to marketing messages from the days of our earliest memories. We know when we're being sold. What we want is for people to be genuine and real—especially at church.

Churches come in all shapes and sizes and meet in all kinds of locations. I have done church in a furniture store, a hotel ballroom, a middle-school cafetorium, an old-fashioned church with a steeple, and a building we designed and built from scratch.

Buildings create expectations, but people always remember how you make them feel. You can be friendly at any location. You can love and serve the next generation. You can help struggling marriages. You can build and develop big people.

Few people understand this better than Steve Chesnut. He and his wife, Gabrielle, were our first guests when we launched Milestone Church. He has grown and helped us improve every step along the way.

He is uniquely gifted to help people connect, to anticipate challenges, and to make the most of their environment. He understands the value in helping every person have every opportunity for meaningful connection. Over the years, I have had the opportunity to sit and talk with so many incredible leaders in the Body of Christ, and I can truly say that I don't know of anyone out there more qualified or who has more insight on this topic than Steve.

We have found that people love good preaching, that they appreciate authentic worship, but nothing bonds them to their church like genuine relationships. While so many things in our world continue to change, one of the things that remains constant is the human need to be seen, known, and loved.

That's what this book is all about. I pray God will use this book to help you and your team connect as many people as possible to God's great vision for His Church.

Jeff Little
Lead Pastor
Milestone Church

INTRODUCTION

LET'S START HERE

Think back to your middle-school cafeteria experience: the smells, the activity—the dread of every new kid. If you spent most of your childhood years in the same town, you may not have experienced this in its heightened torturous form, so let me explain.

Over the course of years, little lunch-table tribes form, merge, and divide, but their relative core stays the same. These groups bond around shared history, hobbies, athletics, arts, neighborhoods, and even trouble.

When you are the new kid, you have about a five-minute window while standing in the lunch line to survey the landscape and choose your people. You don't really care what gets slopped on your tray, because a life-altering decision is looming just beyond the cashier. You do not want to get this wrong.

Then begins the approach. You grab your tray and rapidly scan the room, looking for signals, "friendlies," eye contact, open seats, all while looking as cool as possible but panicking internally.

I know this all too well, having started new middle schools in two different states and new high schools in three. I always hoped for the day when someone saw me and said, "Hey, new kid, come sit with us." It never happened.

I am sure you can relate to the emotions of a new kid's lunch-room experience. This same scenario plays out in almost every station of life—new job, neighborhood, gym, school, club, or church. When coming into a new environment, all we really want is someone who's already connected in the environment to connect to us.

This is especially true in our churches. As time goes by, new be-comes old and we quickly forget what it felt like our first time. We forget what it felt like to not know everything we know that gives us trust and everyone we know who gives us belonging. When you get to the "inside" of something, you can quickly for-get what it felt like to be on the "outside."

As a pastor, church staff member, or lay leader, it is important we stay acquainted with the anxieties and needs of the new per-son. When you put yourself in another's shoes, you are more prone to invite them into your world. But remember, it takes focus, because your world is good, your table is full, you have a group. This book is written to help us all keep looking up to say, "Come sit with us!"

Living for others and for outsiders is not easy. In fact, this may shock you, but I am not a natural connector. I'm really an intro-vert and am prone to selfishly withdraw in social settings. How-ever, anyone who knows me would be surprised to hear that, because it's not how I live. God saved me and called me to love people, so by His grace I do my best to do just that.

There are people who are naturally gifted, but that's not the majority, and that may or may not be you. I want to help people see that connection is not just an action but an attribute. You can choose to connect out of your love for God and love for people. Like kindness, empathy, compassion, and grace, connection exerts God's value on others. We must connect to share God's love.

Opportunities are around all of the time for God to use us. In your church, there may be a prodigal who's returned home, a single-mom looking for a little help, an addict who got buzzed just to get there, or a family just relocated by work or military service. There may be someone making a final search for hope before succumbing to their depression, someone there because their spouse is leaving if they don't change, or the one who's there because their spouse just left. There could be a young couple coming back to church because they want their kids to have morals. Perhaps it's a regular attendee doing life alone and looking for friends. Or it could be someone who just prayed that God would send someone their way, and there you are.

> I want to help people see that connection is not just an action but an attribute.

These are the stories I hear every weekend when I meet people at church. My greatest desire is that every person who attends your church or mine would have a meaningful connection with a person sitting or passing near them. I hope they feel welcomed, valued, and loved in our environments regardless of who they are, what they've done, or how long they've been coming. And connection is for every person in the church, not just the first-time guest.

The many opportunities to connect may feel overwhelming, but the Holy Spirit is there to help us and guide us. You may not be a natural connector, but you can be a supernatural connector. It doesn't matter if your church has tens, hundreds, or thousands of people. It's easy to make it small when you ask God to open your eyes to see who's around you. Who are the ones God is highlighting to you today?

Now imagine a church where every leader came to church thinking of "the one"—it may be the person sitting beside them in the worship service, standing next to them in line for coffee, or simply walking alongside them on the way to a classroom. That person is someone's child, someone's spouse, someone's friend. For years this person may have been prayed for, and now you can be part of an answer to these prayers. One day it may be the one we've been praying for.

I would love to think that at any church, at any time, anyone walking in would feel welcomed and accepted as they come through the doors. Over time these little inconspicuous connections lead to people being known, knowing Jesus, and discovering their place in a growing church family. What life-changing places our churches can be!

It's Good to Meet You

It would be odd to start a book on connection without first

connecting with you. While I hope for the opportunity to know you better, let me share a little about my journey that has produced in me a passion to see people connected in the local church.

In middle school, I started a series of moves around the country from Florida to Texas to South Carolina and back to Florida. I moved to Tennessee for college and Texas for grad school. Every move there was a new school, church, and culture. Every new friend, classroom, and lunchroom (the worst) furthered my education in connection. Some lessons came easy and some came the hard way.

Moving often and visiting new churches marked me as a kid. Our geographically and relationally disjointed family of six would show up at a church Welcome Kiosk and put our lives in the hands of the volunteer on deck. These volunteers we met would walk us to Sunday school classrooms, introduce us to teachers, and ease our nerves with chit-chat along the way. In the coming weeks, these connection volunteers were the ones who remembered me, knew my story, and high-fived me in the hall. These church volunteers would become my heroes.

Fast forward to 2002—my wife, Gabrielle, and I were some of the first guests at Milestone Church, a church plant in Keller, Texas, a Dallas-Fort Worth suburb. That first Sunday we met the lead pastor, Jeff Little, and his wife, Brandy. They invited us to dinner that very next week to intentionally connect with us. Our hearts resonated as we heard the vision God had given them for a dynamic local church that would impact a region for Christ. We signed on that first week, and the second Sunday Pastor Jeff put us in charge of greeting and connecting the new guests. (I guess at that point we'd been there twice as long as them!)

I remember the value of someone connecting with us, caring about us, learning about us, and inviting us into what God was doing through this church. From that second week until now, I have tried to create the same experience for every person coming behind us. It's now been several years and with several thousands in weekend attendance at multiple campuses, the team has grown, our processes have changed, but the heart is still the same. God's heart for people burns in our lead pastor, in me, in our team, and throughout our church family.

A final thing about me: as I said earlier, I am an introvert. While I have grown to be more natural at connecting, I could not do it without a supernatural cause and supernatural help. I connect because people matter to God, and relationships are how He builds His Church. I push myself into it; I work at it. All that to say, if I can do it, so can you.

Where We're Headed

In this book, I will share the *power of connection* and why it's so important to the culture of your church. I'll break down the *principles of connection* so that you can see that it's not just a personality but something that you and your teams can replicate. And finally, I'll share about a *process of connection* that moves people from being first-time guests to becoming active members who are growing in Jesus, building meaningful relationships, and making a difference.

Just like a good connection process, this entire book moves from a broad to a narrow audience. As you read, you'll find more and more practical tools to implement. Everyone should be inspired by the power of connection, key leaders and church staff can live out the principles in section two, and the final section on process is written specifically with church leadership in mind.

I know your context is likely different from mine (size, location, atmosphere, denomination, church age, etc.). What I will share in this book are connection keys I've personally lived and found to be successful in many different contexts. In writing this, I have consulted several of the best connectors I know from various denominations and regions to hopefully be able to help you in your context.

I would not say I am an expert, but I would say I am extremely experienced. As I have been invited to share my experience with other pastors and church leaders, they've asked me to write about these principles that have impacted them personally and the people they serve. My goal is that what they may have learned firsthand, you can learn from this book and pass it along to those you lead.

In the final chapter, I'll share with you the "secret recipe" that I'd love not to be a secret. For many years now, we've used an intentional process of taking pictures of each person who becomes part of our church and posting them on the People Board wall in our office. We keep their faces in front of us for an entire year to help us remember their names and their stories and to help them take spiritual steps. I hope it inspires you.

That's where we're going, and I'm so glad you care about people enough to invest time into reading this book. I hope to impart to you my passion to see people connect in the local church. I don't think there is anything that compares to the fullness of life that comes from a connection to Jesus and a connection to spiritual family through the local church. By God's grace we get to help people find both of these.

SECTION I

THE POWER OF CONNECTION

WHY connection is the
church-culture game changer

(For Everyone in the Church)

SECTION II

THE PRINCIPLES OF CONNECTION

WHAT you can do to be
a better connector

(For Volunteers & Leadership)

SECTION III

THE PROCESS OF CONNECTION

HOW to build a
connection process

(For Leadership)

THE POWER OF CONNECTION

**To Spotlight the People; To Start Relationships;
To Show Kindness; To Open Doors of Opportunity;
To Reach the Community**

The key to the power of connection is the simplicity of the concept but the profoundness of its impact. It's easy to overlook. We see the effect we like, but connection is often the cause we don't think of. Many do it casually, but with intentionality the impact can be exponential.

There is power in connection to radically impact someone's life. We are all one connection away from an opportunity that enlarges our own life. When we increase our connections, we enrich our lives and the lives of others.

The power of connection is displayed in the forming of relationships, the shaping of the culture of churches, and the God-honoring effects of focused kindness in our world. It makes for a greater culture in the church and invites the outside culture to the church.

1

TO SPOTLIGHT THE PEOPLE

*Each of you should use whatever gift you have
received to serve others, as faithful stewards of
God's grace in its various forms.*

1 PETER 4:10, NIV

Worship is worship. Preaching is preaching. Programs are programs. The church is the people—remarkable people using their gifts to create an irresistible environment that displays the grace of God in its various forms. It is powerful when God works through a gifted individual leading from the stage, but what I love the most is when God works through the gifted people sitting in the seats.

Several years and thousands of changed lives ago, my wife, Gabrielle, and I were the first guests at Milestone Church's grand opening service in October 2002. It was in a middle-school cafetorium, with childcare in the halls, the smell of fish sticks in the air, and Jesus being preached from a short stage. We didn't come back for the production, preaching, or programs; we came back for the people and the vision they invited us into.

What if the people came back for the people? It's wild to think, but one of the greatest draws to the future church will simply be the people. I know this should be obvious because that is what the local church has always been—a gathering. But more than a gathering of people, it's a gathering of God's people with open doors and open arms to everyone.

We are programmed by our Creator with a longing to be known and that's not going away regardless of technological capabilities. It's biology. We can know a lot of content and connect online, but there is a void if we do not know God and aren't known by a family. The local church *has* the answers and *is* the answer to this longing.

You can't download church, podcast church, or google church—you are a part of the church. It's a gathering of people growing in grace. It's a gathering to worship in Jesus' name and invite the transforming presence of God to do what only He can do in our lives. The local church is the answer to the pains of our world—past, present, and most certainly future.

> The church
> is the people.

More and more, people will be drawn to caring churches, looking for authentic people who embrace them. It seems so simple now, but it will become increasingly profound. People will realize there is a place they can go and interact with authentic people without transaction—a place where they can discover truth, be encouraged, and find hope and help in life. Attending your church should be the highlight of someone's week.

The church is only growing in relevance in our ever-advancing world. Technology hasn't replaced our need for physical social connectedness; it has highlighted its importance in our lives. As our world accelerates in online social engagement, the anxiety and loneliness epidemic is growing out of control. It was a fun experiment in technology, but people are realizing they need connection with real people. As Ben Sasse said so well in his book *Them*, "We're hyperconnected, and disconnected." Sasse goes on to reflect on the data analyzed by Duke University's social scientist Miller McPherson:

> More alarmingly, the number of Americans who count no friends at all—no one in whom they confide about important matters, no one with whom they share life's joys and burdens—has soared. In the mid-2000s, one quarter of Americans said they had no one with whom to talk about things that matter. That was triple the percentage from the 1980s. These trends have not slowed.[1]

Loneliness and depression are destroying countless lives in our world today, but the local church is the answer. People will walk into churches looking for a friend—and find Jesus and His family. They will be looking for answers in life and will find the way, the truth, and the life. Growing churches will be churches that know how to connect people to people, not just host people in large groups.

My hope each week is that when people sit for a meal after church, the conversation turns toward their worship experience—that they remark on the presence of God and the amazing people they interacted with: the volunteers, the staff, the person who sat beside them and made them feel special and welcome. Because that is what remarkable is: people "re-marking" on what they felt.

I recently heard my favorite scenario play out: a family at a restaurant for lunch talking about their experience at Milestone and how people went out of their way to love them. They were "re-marking" on the amazing people, not the building, flowers, music, sermon—the people! Every time I hear this, it makes me so grateful for our people and how they love like Jesus.

An area pastor mentioned to me that he had visited our church on his summer sabbatical break. He and his wife walked in and immediately felt something different. He told me it didn't go unnoticed to his nineteen-year-old son, who said, "Dad, there is something different about the people." He went on trying to articulate an authenticity, an engagement, a connection he felt.

This is the highest compliment you can pay to any church, or any pastor, in my opinion. The church is the people, the gathering of believers. It's the Body and Bride of Christ. If we are going to brag about anything, let's brag about Jesus' bride.

In the early days of Milestone Church, we would host an event about every six weeks called *Newcomers*. People new to the church would have dessert and coffee with Pastor Jeff and Brandy, our small staff team, and key volunteers. It was so valuable because we were able to meet those new to the environment and ask them what they enjoy about the church. We tried to phrase it as subtly as possible but the question was basically, "So . . . why do you keep coming back?" I loved hearing the feedback.

In one *Newcomers* event the prevailing theme was the great preaching, then the next was the powerful worship, and the student ministry got an occasional shout-out. I remember sitting in one of those events thinking, *What if they were so well served and loved, the response on the top of their minds was not just great preaching, worship, and kids' ministry, but the amazing people they encountered?*

Now, here we are several intentional years later and I'm in awe of how many times I hear remarks about our people every weekend. Honestly, maybe I hear it more often now because great preaching, worship, and kids' ministry are typically expected. But let me tell you what's not expected:

- Someone knowing you are new and going out of their way to help you feel welcomed

- The person sitting beside you being genuinely interested in who you are

- A Small Group leader going out of their way to invite you to their group

- A prayer team member who doesn't just pray for you but follows up with and takes care of you

- Someone who disagrees with you and your choices but still loves you and accepts you

All of that may not be expected, but together we can change that. I think it *should* be expected of the local church—simply valuing, serving, and connecting with each person just as Jesus would.

Michael's Experience

Recently I met a first-time guest at our church named Michael. His family had just moved to the area and a coworker invited them to Milestone. After the service was over, the friend who invited Michael brought him up to me, introduced me, and asked him to share his feedback with me.

Michael told me that this was the best church experience he'd ever had. And due to work transfers, he'd had a lot of them. From guest parking to child check-in, hosting, and hospitality, he said it was as good as he'd seen or experienced anywhere, not just "church." Wow! What a compliment! I am so proud of our people, and I was excited for an even bigger reason—this should be everyone's experience, including the one coming to church for the very first time. Think about that. The church can be the most engaging, loving, hospitable, friendly environment that someone has ever been in.

No matter the size of your church, people want to know they matter. People matter to God, so we need to make sure they know they matter to us. So many churches feel this but don't show it. People don't *know* you care until you *show* you care (for them).

People don't drive by your church and know there is a group of people inside who care about them. You know you care, but how would they know that? It's interesting when you think about it from their perspective. We just assume they know we care because we *do* care, but that is not enough.

Do you think the restaurant down the street, or library, or gym cares about you? No. We don't think anything more of their concern for us than that they'd love our business—that is, until we connect with the people in those buildings and they can demonstrate a deeper value by serving us in a way that supersedes our expectations.

> The church can be the most engaging, loving, hospitable, friendly environment that someone has ever been in.

We need to constantly remind ourselves that people don't know what we feel on the inside. They can't see our heart, motives, or intentions. They see what we do for them. We get into the most trouble when we assume that those we love and value know that we love and value them, even when we've done nothing to communicate that we do. People do not feel what you feel for them; they feel what you *do* for them.

I remember hearing a story of a lady who drove by our church week after week noticing the parking team out in the heat, cold, and rain. She commented that when she saw them consistently smiling and serving people, she thought, *Whatever they have, I need.* She eventually came in and found Jesus!

Another gentleman named Dale stopped by when our interns did a free coffee drive-thru in the church parking lot. He had driven by the building many times, considered himself agnostic, but seeing people serving like Jesus sent him on a journey to find a relationship with Jesus for himself.

I heard about another person who spent weeks sitting in his car in the parking lot, afraid to come in. He was afraid that he'd be rejected at the doors. I am so glad our parking team was so kind to him. When he finally came in, he was warmly welcomed as he received the embrace of Jesus and His Church.

> People do not feel what you feel for them; they feel what you do for them.

Serving one another with our gifts undeniably communicates our value for people. Every weekend, each extroverted act of service—connecting with people from the parking lot to the worship center and back again—is reinforcing God's value for people. Even without a word, an environment of people using their gifts communicates their heart for people, the heart of the church, and ultimately the heart of God.

A Five-Star Experience for Everyone

I was raised in the hospitality industry. Restaurants, hotels, resorts were literally second homes growing up. As long as I can remember, I've been a customer-service geek. I get so excited about people strategically and creatively finding little ways to connect through service. Hospitality is more than a description of an industry; it's an instruction from the Bible.

> *Above all, love each other deeply,*
> *because love covers over a*
> *multitude of sins. Offer <u>hospitality</u> to*
> *one another without grumbling.*
> **I PETER 4:8-9, NIV**

> *Share with the Lord's people who are in need.*
> *Practice <u>hospitality</u>.*
> **ROMANS 12:13, NIV**

> *Do not forget to show <u>hospitality</u> to strangers,*
> *for by so doing some people have shown*
> *<u>hospitality</u> to angels without knowing it.*
> **HEBREWS 13:2, NIV**

It's the small things that communicate that we anticipated someone's need before it became one, answered a question before it was thought to be asked, and customized an experience tailored to the individual. These speak volumes. I even get excited about the problems we solve that make it an even greater experience for the individual than if the problem had never occurred. I encourage our team to take an "ow" and make it a "wow!"

Great customer service is simply the intentional efforts a business makes to create a meaningful connection with their customers. It creates "the feels," and it's that impression (not just the product) that makes them want to return. These meaningful connections are especially important these days when you are able to get any product online, including church services.

Think about this for a minute: Isn't it interesting that the highest-quality customer service usually goes to the highest-paying customer? I am not against paying for great service; in fact I love it. But it's crazy that the people with the highest dollar value get the highest esteemed value. Those who potentially need it least receive it most.

I've enjoyed staying at high-end resorts and eating at high-end restaurants. The service at these places is often exceptional. But then I have the thought, *These employees, although great and hospitable, are getting paid to treat me well and to make me feel special. They get paid to say, "Yes, sir, Mr. Chesnut."*

Now catch this: We, the church, have the opportunity to build environments that make everyone feel five-star valued—for free. No matter a person's economic status, age, or appearance, they can come in the doors of our church and get treated like royalty. We can treat them better than anywhere on the planet, and it's completely free. That's how it should feel when you come into God's house.

I am not discrediting anyone in the customer-service industry or questioning authenticity. Many leaders in this industry inspire me. I believe that the best of the best are where they are because of a genuine value for people and a heart to serve others. The motivation can come from a different place and impact people in an entirely non-transactional way when it comes from God.

Maya Angelou once said, "I've learned that people will forget what you said, people will forget what you did, but people will never forget how you made them feel."[2]

The Standard in Customer Service

I believe the local church should set the industry standard for customer service. And that is not some hyperbolic language. I mean it 100 percent. More than any other industry, we are in the people-serving business. Jesus, our servant leader and Lord, gave His life for the church and made serving the way to greatness in His Kingdom. He then filled us with His Holy Spirit, and with His love flowing through us, there is just no way the world can compete.

Since everything good comes from God, I am not too proud to learn from customer-service industry leaders like Disney, Chick-fil-A, Nordstrom, and the Ritz-Carlton. These are some great customer-service companies. I have applied so many things to the local church that I first learned from them.

I recently attended the Ritz-Carlton customer-service symposium. It was a wonderful time of training as I learned many of the key motivators and core values shared by their "ladies and gentlemen" who create the Ritz-Carlton culture. The founder and visionary of this amazing culture is a man named Horst Schulze. I love what he shares in *Excellence Wins* about the power of connection in the church:

> When you walk into a church, you naturally expect the

preaching to be biblical (no defects). You expect the service to start and end at the stated hours (timeliness). But along the way, does anyone notice you—anyone, that is, besides the official "greeters" who have been told to do so? Does a pastor or elder look you in the eye and smile or shake your hand? Are you made to feel that you matter in some small way to this large and busy institution . . . Worshippers come to connect with God, of course. But they'd also like to connect with a fellow human being or two. As the wise and beloved nineteenth-century British preacher Joseph Parker is reported to have once said, "There is a broken heart in every pew."[3]

I want the church to be leading in people-serving because we represent the people-serving leader—Jesus. "Who, being in very nature God, did not consider equality with God something to be used to his own advantage; rather, he made himself nothing by taking the very nature of a servant" (Philippians 2:6-7a, NIV).

I hope a day comes when the customer-service leaders in your region are coming to your church to learn how you serve people so well. They will be inspired by the excellence and enthusiasm coming from your volunteers, those not even paid to be this great. How incredible this must be for someone coming in from the outside.

Let's blow minds. The message of Jesus is mind-blowing; it's *Good News* for all people. Our message is extraordinary, so why shouldn't people feel extraordinary the moment they come onto our church campus? We'll show them that Jesus is the extra in our ordinary.

Heart Connection Is in the Second Mile

You've likely heard the common saying "Go the second mile." I have heard individuals, coaches, and even companies use it to motivate. I love it, but what does it mean to go the second mile?

It started with the famous words of Jesus: "If anyone forces you to go one mile, go with them two miles" (Matthew 5:41, NIV). You see, the first mile in this context was not optional. It was the responsibility of a Jewish civilian to carry the supplies of a Roman soldier for one mile upon request. However, what Jesus is saying is, "Don't just do the obligatory or the expected; go a second mile too." This is pretty radical because it could set you off on a 4-mile round trip of inconvenience.

As you can imagine, the second mile is where the question gets asked, "Why are you doing this? We passed the mile marker just back there." All of a sudden, the one serving is in the position of guiding the terms of this arrangement and establishing their dignity. The second mile provokes the key question Jesus is after: What would motivate someone to do this?

The way I think about it is this: The first mile is for you, but the second mile is for Jesus. In this second mile, you are going to see the Jesus in me. In this second mile, you are going to begin to feel something you've never felt before. Only a revelation of God's love could fuel such motivation, and that motivation becomes apparent.

When we move past the established transactional service norms, we enter a new space of connection. We are no

15

longer just connecting to an outcome; we are connecting with a person. Whatever the scenario is, there is generally a first-mile expectation that is obvious. But when you take the same scenario and go the second mile with it, it is connecting with the heart.

I don't know if there is an environment more expected to deliver on this value for people than the church. I think in terms of mile one being a standard of service, and mile two really showing the heart behind it. Here are some examples of taking a few customary standards to the second mile:

FIRST MILE *(EXPECTED)*	→	SECOND MILE *(UNEXPECTED)*
KINDNESS	→	KNOWN BY NAME
FRIENDLINESS	→	A FRIEND
EXCELLENCE	→	AUTHENTICITY
EFFICIENCY	→	ANTICIPATION
SAFETY	→	PEACE
PROCESS	→	PERSONALIZATION

Going the second mile will always take more time and energy. This extra effort is where a real heart for connections begins to distinguish itself from casual friendliness. Passing that one-mile marker is a distinct difference in the culture of an environment that few pursue. As famously quoted by legendary Dallas Cowboys quarterback Roger Staubach, "There are no traffic jams along the extra mile."

Welcome-Box Impact

For many years now, Milestone Church has delivered high-value Welcome Boxes to people who move to our community. Hundreds of custom-designed boxes are delivered every year that include an impressive coffee tumbler, fun treats, other "wow" stuff, and clear information on how we are here to serve them. Before they ever come to us, we want people in the community to see we are willing to go the second, third, and fourth mile to come to them. It's a lifeline we throw, and they can pull on it as needed. And many do.

Recently a woman named Lisa sent in a handwritten letter to express her gratitude for the Welcome Box. She went on to explain that she and her husband both enjoyed the coffee tumbler so much that they fight over it every morning. One morning, after months of competing for the tumbler, they had the funny thought that she decided to communicate with us. "We've been loving and fighting over this tumbler so much, maybe we should check out the church?" The letter went on to say they have been visiting for several weeks and are loving it.

That's mile one. So what's the second mile? When I saw the note, my first thought was probably the same as yours, and our team: Let's send them a second mug so they don't have to share it, and let's invite them to the next membership class to get them plugged in. We don't just want them attending; we want them to take steps, grow spiritually, and get connected.

Sure enough, they got the second mug with a handwritten note inviting them to attend Discovery 101, the first class in our Growth Track (more on this in chapter 14). They attended, joined, and sent an email to the church letting us know how grateful they were for the second-mile service.

FROM: LISA
SUBJECT: THANK YOU!
TO: MILESTONE

Each time we visit, we continue to be impressed with Milestone Church. The people who, on their own, move to the center so those arriving later can have the end seats. The busy pastors with microphones on their way to the front stopping to greet us. The staff who don't let people "fall through the cracks" and had our signup sheets for the 201 class (that were turned in after Discovery 101 on Sunday afternoon) inputted and confirmed by email Monday morning. Also, the people who spend time responding in a personal way to emails. Thank you.

In a time when electronic communication is the norm, it is a treat to get real handwritten non-junk mail. Thank you for the gift cards, and for the box FedEx delivered last week containing another thermal cup and handwritten note. Your generosity and genuine care for people are admirable and God keeps confirming that Milestone is a place He wants us to worship and work.

Thank you for all the things you are doing right.

Lisa and Mark

Beyond the gratitude for the thermal cup, I love that she sees the bigger heart behind it all. She's experiencing all of the second-mile efforts to help her and her husband feel welcomed and loved in our environment. From years of seeing this, I know her experience will not stop with her, that now she will reciprocate in our environment and maybe even join the Welcome Box team.

Connection Is Attractional

A great culture of connection makes up for a lot of exterior shortcomings. Our church was 15 years old before there was any curb appeal. I look back at where we were, what we wore, and what we did, and I think, *It's a good thing we were relational because we sure weren't attractional.*

This was part of God's plan for the story of Milestone. Pastor Jeff did not feel his calling was to be a superstar but rather a supercoach. The decision early on was to focus on raising up great people in order to build on transferable values, not just the special giftings of a few. It's a model that can be reproduced because it's built on the people and the gifts in them, not just the giftedness of the senior leader. I am so grateful for a pastor with this vision.

The reason my wife and I came back to Milestone after our first visit was because we got connected to relationships and a vision we were passionate about—not because it was cool. But it turns out, in the long run, growing spiritually, walking in our calling, and living for a shared purpose with friends is pretty cool.

When I look around at so many churches these days, I am amazed how environmentally attractional they are. Even these new church plants have incredible vision to retrofit cafeterias and movie theaters into amazing environments. This is awesome and should be pursued with great creativity. My only suggestion would be to make sure you put as much energy into the development of attractional people, not just attractional environments. I like to think, *If the power went out, would we still be cool?*

A person might come to your church for inspiring productions and excellent programs, but they stay for the people. They stay for the relationships. In the next chapter, I will share with you the power of connection to start relationships.

Key Takeaways

- The church is the people.
- We can know a lot of content and connect online, but there is a void if we do not know God and aren't known by family.
- People are drawn to caring churches with authentic people who embrace them.
- The church can be the most engaging, loving, hospitable, friendly environment that someone has ever been in.
- People don't *know* you care until you *show* you care (for them).
- People do not feel what you feel for them; they feel what you *do* for them.
- Local churches have the opportunity to build environments that make everyone feel five-star valued.
- The second mile provokes the key question Jesus is after: What would motivate someone to do this?

Reflection Questions

1. Do you believe the local church can be the most life-giving environment someone has ever been in?
2. How can you get better at showing you care about people who come to your church?
3. How can you go the second mile for someone today and show them the love of Jesus?

2

TO START RELATIONSHIPS

*For God so loved the world that he gave his
one and only Son, that whoever believes in
him shall not perish but have eternal life.*

JOHN 3:16, NIV

We know God's love because He chose to connect with us. God did not only love the world He created, but He also connected to it. He started the relationship. God was the first to connect. The connection came in the form of His Son, Jesus, who became one of us, thus writing Himself into the story of His own creation. He then died on the cross in our place to save us from our sins. Then having rose from the dead, He sent His Holy Spirit to constantly connect with us.

In His years on Earth, Jesus was the ultimate connector. He walked through a town and, with a few conversations, gathered a group of friends who would change the world. "Come follow me," Jesus called to two fishermen, Peter and Andrew, and they left their business and joined Him. They went along, saw James and John, and Jesus called them as well. They too followed Jesus.[4]

Before these guys knew what was going on, they and others had joined Jesus' Small Group, started discipleship in His Growth Track, and signed up for the Volunteer Team. Soon they'd put on incredible services, ushered groups of 5,000+ people, and provided hospitality to feed them.[5] Peter even became the self-appointed head of Jesus' safety team.[6]

One connection to Jesus forever changed the disciples' lives and eternities. They went from being some obscure fishermen to some of the most famous men in history—men entrusted with the Great Commission in Matthew 28:19: "Therefore go and make disciples of all nations, baptizing them in the name of the Father and of the Son and of the Holy Spirit" (NIV). That's the power of connection.

This power is magnified when centered on the Great Commission and partnered with Jesus to build His Church. Connection in the church is the catalyst of outreach, discipleship, and meaningful, authentic relationships. It is the others-focused, servant-minded, sacrificial giving of relational and emotional energy that creates the beautiful picture we see in Acts 2. They still needed to grow in inclusivity, but they were beginning to thrive relationally in this new community of faith.

> *All the believers were together and had*
> *everything in common. They sold property and*
> *possessions to give to anyone who had need. Every*
> *day they continued to meet together in the temple*
> *courts. They broke bread in their homes and ate*
> *together with glad and sincere hearts, praising*
> *God and enjoying the favor of all the people. And*

the Lord added to their number daily those who
were being saved.

ACTS 2:44-47, NIV

You have to connect to build a family, and that's what God is building. God sets the lonely in families (see Psalm 68:6), builds His Church (see Matthew 16:18), arranges each member in the Body as He wants them (see 1 Corinthians 12:18), and connects living stones together to build a spiritual house (see 1 Peter 2:5).

Connectors Are Relationship Starters

Just like the disciples were impacted by Jesus' invitation, one small connection can make an eternal difference in a person's life. It can change the trajectory of a life and open a whole new door of opportunity to an individual. Think about it: Who introduced you to your spouse? Your career opportunity? Your newest hobby? Your church? Aren't you grateful they didn't just mind their own business or keep to themselves?

Connectors demonstrate value for people. Many feel it, but the connector acts on it. They initiate contact by saying hello, putting out their hand, and striking up a conversation. They take the risk and others simply reciprocate. But take the connector out of this relational exchange and the pieces just don't come together.

Connectors highlight the who behind the what and bring significance to any interaction or environment. Connectors turn our world from being transactional to being relational.

Relationships are our highest human value and connection is the starting point. Connectors are the brokers of relationships, friendships, and in the church, spiritual family.

In Section II, I will give you the practicals on how you can do this well by:

- Being the first to connect
- Knowing who to connect to
- Knowing what to say
- Overcoming rejection
- Remembering names
- Adding value to people

—

Several years back, I was at the pre-season coaches meeting for my son's six-year-old basketball team. I walked into a room predominantly full of other dads like me from our community. As a connector, a Christian, and a pastor, this is like fishing in a stocked pond. But this night, I didn't want to fish; I didn't want to talk to anyone. I found an open seat at a table and just sat there. I didn't make eye contact, didn't say hello, didn't smile. It was totally out of my norm. But that night wasn't the norm. That night I had the stomach bug. I think I did a good job of hiding it on the outside, but it took everything I had to keep it on the inside.

As I drove home from the meeting, sipping my Sprite, I had a crazy revelation: nobody introduced themselves to me. This left me a little discouraged, only to lead me to a more depressing thought: *Has anyone ever introduced themselves to me?*

As I began to unravel this fever-heightened pity-party, I was stunned by the realization that no, people don't introduce themselves to me, and no, I could not think of a time when someone has walked up and introduced themselves to me. What's wrong with me? Why don't people like me? You can imagine the insecurity I felt. Then I figured it out. Nobody introduces themselves to me because I've already introduced myself to them.

> Connectors turn our world from being transactional to being relational.

Had I been my best living-on-mission self that night, my quiet coaches table would have all met each other, laughed a little, learned what each other did for a living, and shared how long they'd been in the area. I would have learned how long their boys have played basketball. I would have subtly gotten a gauge on where they are in regards to faith or church involvement.

The next time these men saw me or each other, they'd say hello and welcome the familiar faces and easy interaction. We would introduce our wives and our kids and enjoy the sense of being known in a new environment. That's what would have happened because that's what a connector naturally does.

As a connector, you have the power to spark relationships in whatever environment you are in. All it takes is one person reaching out to get others to open up. Think about it this way: Most people see others as wearing a "Closed" sign around their neck—closed to dialogue, closed to eye contact, closed to relationship, closed to human interaction. But a connector (with appropriate awareness) sees "Open." As soon as a connector reaches out, the "Closed" sign flips, and as you look around, others start flipping their signs to "Open" as well.

Going back to the sick-stomach, anti-social coaches meeting— it turns out the person I sat next to ended up becoming a dear friend of mine. However, the friendship didn't come about until two years later when our boys were on a baseball team together and I got a second chance to connect—a connection redo.

Relationships = Happiness

When we connect people to one another or make a connection ourselves, we bring happiness into their lives and our own. We may have thought it was the new car, bigger house, or more money that brought us happiness. But really, what brings us the most joy is relational connectedness.

In his book *The Art of Connection,* Michael J. Gelb cites multiple studies that come back to the same conclusion: Meaningful social connections make your life better, and when you're better, you make others better.

> Psychiatrist and professor at Harvard Medical School Robert J. Waldinger is the current director of the Laboratory of Adult Development at Massachusetts General Hospital, where he

oversees the world's longest-running study of happiness. For more than seventy-seven years the lab has followed a group of 724 men, measuring the factors that most influence their mental and physical health.

Waldinger and his three predecessors all found that most younger men believe that money, power, achievement, and fame are the keys to success and happiness. That's certainly the impression one gets from contemporary media, advertising, video games, and reality television. But the results of the study are undeniably clear: the most important factor in a happy and healthy life is a positive sense of connection with others.[7]

I think we'd all agree with this study. We already know it in our core. Yet we tend to still get distracted from building meaning-ful connections and settling for the lesser things in life.

In the same way, I know nutritious food will make me feel good and junk food will make me feel bad. But it still takes work and energy to choose what is best for me. Unfortunately, social me-dia connectedness has become the junk food of real relational connectedness. It tastes good, and it's fine in moderation, but we sure don't want to make it our primary sustenance.

We can easily be connecting digitally and miss the real-life new friendship at the table, the one that will bring a real sense of happiness. Algorithms help us know who to like and follow on-line, but in real life we need connectors to start the dialogues that cause people to set their phones down. We need more peo-ple reaching out, introducing themselves, and opening up a new world of relationships.

There is one thing our increasingly digital age cannot produce: the person who cares about you and brings you soup when you are sick. A delivery service might get the soup to you, but they sure aren't going to care enough to sit with you or check on you. That's where happiness is found, and connectors help people find this happiness.

Ralph Waldo Emerson said, "It is one of the most beautiful compensations of this life that no man can sincerely try to help another without helping himself."[8]

Networking Is Transactional; Connecting Is Relational

Networking is a transactional, self-serving method to increase your relational capital. It is not the same as connecting. Networking is transactional; connecting is relational with the intention to serve others. Networking is for you; connecting is for others.

I'm sure you've been in those awkward scenarios where business cards start flying around and everyone is nervously shaking hands while looking out for the better opportunity over your shoulder.

Not fun. I've been there and done that. I can still recall that dirty sense of striving, pushing, and trying to make something happen. So you may be saying, "Then how do you get yourself out there?" Good news! There is a better way—connecting, and it's not just semantics.

Connection is not networking with others; it's serving others. Great connectors are genuinely looking to help someone else, not themselves. Serving others is where the real connections are made. Helping someone solve their problems, reach their potential, accomplish their purpose, or simply feel a part of the church is the power of connection.

> Networking is transactional; connecting is relational with the intention to serve others.

Connection starts with the premise of adding value to someone else, not increasing your own value. Think of the people who have given you a great first impression. They walked away and you thought, *I like that person.* Odds are they were looking to add value to you in some way. They talked less of themselves and asked more about you.

That's ultimately what a great connector does. They aren't just friendly to you. They make you feel like a real friend.

A generous person will prosper; whoever refreshes others will be refreshed.
PROVERBS 11:25, NIV

Key Takeaways

- We know God's love because He chose to connect with us.
- One small connection can make an eternal difference in a person's life.
- Connectors demonstrate value for people. Many feel it, but the connector acts on it.
- Meaningful social connections with others provide our greatest sense of happiness.
- Connectors turn our world from being transactional to relational.
- Networking is transactional; connecting is relational with the intention to serve others.
- Connectors aren't just friendly to you; they make you feel like a real friend.

Reflection Questions

1. What did God have to do for us to know His love for us?
2. What is the difference between networking and connecting?
3. Do people around you just think of you as friendly or do they think you're a friend?

3

TO SHOW KINDNESS

*Do nothing out of selfish ambition or
vain conceit. Rather, in humility value
others above yourself, not looking to your own
interests but each of you to the interests
of the others.*

PHILIPPIANS 2:3-4, NIV

I know who you are. I see you on stage" was the abrupt greeting I got from a young cashier named Carley as I stepped up to order my lunch at a local restaurant. She said it so matter-of-factly, it caught me off guard. Her numb tone and lack of pretense grabbed my attention. I immediately had compassion for her and could tell there was a lot of pain in her life.

A few minutes later, I came back around to follow up with her and see how I might help her. She explained how her family was broken, her parents were on drugs, and she was living with her aunt and uncle. Her aunt's and uncle's lives were a wreck too, but they had all decided to try church to find some hope.

I'll never forget what she said next. Carley marked me for a lifetime with her words. In her same monotone voice, she said, "I like coming to your church because it is the only place I feel good." It hit me hard. She talked about how people at the doors and people she walked by in the foyer smiled and said hi to her, and how it made her feel good—such simple things.

Understanding all of the pain surrounding her life, her words both broke me and encouraged me all at once. As I drove away praying for this young girl and reflecting on our conversation, I was reminded of what she said. I thought, *Our church is not simply the only place she feels good; it's the only place she feels God.*

All of those enthusiastic parkers, engaging greeters, and people intentionally connecting with kindness are expressing the heart of God to Carley. Every act of focused kindness is an opportunity to show God's love for people, and when Carley's family comes in, they feel it.

I don't ever want us to miss an opportunity to show God's love to the Carleys who come into our church or into our lives. But in order to do that, we need to be focused on the Carleys, by focusing our kindness—because everyone needs kindness.

Connection Is Focused Kindness

I have yet to hear someone say, "You know what? Our church is really unfriendly." Nobody thinks this of their own environment. Even if someone attends the coldest church in the world, you tend to just get thicker skin and adapt to the temperature. It's a blind spot for all of us and an area in which everyone can get better when we become more intentional. Churches do not intend to come across as unfriendly, but many get a bad reputation because they are unfocused.

Several years back, I walked up to say hello to a couple sitting in the worship center before a Sunday service. I smiled and said hello and immediately the wife began to cry. She apologized and explained that this was their second church visit that morning. They had just walked out of a church down the road because someone asked them to move because they were in their seats.

I'm sure this individual who hurt them was not looking to intentionally cause pain, but they were definitely not focused on showing kindness. When we are focused on connecting with people, we see them, are better able to understand what's going on with them, and hopefully can mitigate any unintentional hurt. A simple acknowledgment even in passing is an easy act of kindness that is often overlooked, but with great consequence.

Research done by customer-service experts at the Capella Group discovered the importance of distance in determining how a guest experiences kindness in their hotels. They discovered that if someone comes within about ten feet of another person, a kind greeting is expected.[9] Staff, employees, volunteers, etc., are the ones responsible for carrying the burden of the greeting, not the guest. However, if someone is not acknowledged, it's not a neutral effect in our churches; it's a negative effect.

Anyone wearing a name tag/sticker/lanyard needs to know this. Within ten feet, eye contact and a cordial greeting are expected regardless of personality, responsibility, or urgency of the matter they are hastily solving. It doesn't matter if someone perceives themselves as "simply a volunteer"; when they are wearing that volunteer tag or standing at that door, they may be perceived as the captain of the ship and should steward that influence well.

I often joke with our team and volunteers that they may not see themselves as a big deal—but they are. They are like Mickey Mouse at Disney World. I don't know if you've ever been to the Magic Kingdom, but in his domain, Mickey is the man. He's a rockstar! However, outside of the Magic Kingdom, if someone showed up in a mouse suit, we'd probably call security. Context is key, and staff and volunteers are a big deal inside our churches.

> Most often, bad church experiences are simply unmet expectations.

I constantly remind myself to walk slower, smile, and say hello. Even if I'm in a hurry, simple respect and politeness are more important than any problem I am trying to solve.

The church is one of the few places where personal acknowledgment is still expected. People are not expecting "Do you like that organic milk?" kind of engagement at the grocery store. Nobody says, "Do you want to sit by me?" at the movies. But when they come to your church, they are expecting engagement.

Most often, bad church experiences are simply unmet expectations. Maybe they thought someone would invite them to come and sit with them. They may have even said, "No, thank you" to your offer, but they still felt welcomed that you asked. They don't know about the "no-hassle guarantee"; they just know that nobody talked to them.

Connection is focused kindness. And we need more of it in our world. We're prone to look out for ourselves, but there is something powerful about how a connector has eyes to see others and the compassion to engage with them. We need to genuinely look to serve and not sell—serve others' interests and not our own. When we are able to do that, we establish trust and the influence to connect.

Kindness Creates Connection

Ask yourself this question: What would it take to stop you in mid-stride if you were out for a jog? Would you stop to pick up a penny? A nickel? Maybe stop for a quarter? A dollar? What would it take? The faster our world gets, the more it takes for us to slow down. If there's one thing people will still stop for, it's genuine kindness.

Until you experience a genuine act of kindness personally, you don't really get it. But the first time a stranger goes out of their way or gives their money to pay for your food, your gas, or your coffee, there is an instant connection. It is an indebtedness of compassion where you want to "kind them back."

In a talk on how acts of kindness impact humans, author and speaker Simon Sinek explains the science behind what makes us feel good and connected when providing, receiving, or even witnessing an act of kindness.

> Now in our bodies is a chemical called oxytocin. Oxytocin is responsible for all the warm and fuzzies, unicorns and rainbows. It's responsible for all the warm feelings and connectedness we have with each other—friendship, love. Huge amounts of oxytocin surge through a woman's body as she gives birth. This is what is responsible for the mother-child bond. Oxytocin binds human beings. There are many ways to get oxytocin, one of them is acts of kindness, acts of generosity.[10]

Considering how acts of kindness make people feel, I think they are the best ongoing way for a church to connect with their community and show the love of Jesus. We encourage this at Milestone Church and provide special invite cards to accompany an act of kindness. I love when we get thank-you notes and emails, and when people mention on their first-time guest card how a member's act of kindness led to their visit.

> Kindness builds a bridge of trust that allows for meaningful connection.

Plus, kindness often creates this evangelistic connection without having to talk—no words needed. The gospel must be proclaimed, but I think that seeds of evangelism are quiet acts of kindness that have resounding effects. Think about it: people hardly answer their phones anymore; they aren't generally ready to talk with a stranger until a sincere connection is established.

Kindness builds a bridge of trust that allows for meaningful connection. It is the best way to show our community we sincerely care about them. Once a year, we have something we call "Serve Day" when we mobilize our entire church to serve our community with acts of kindness. We do this through cleaning parks, clearing code violations, serving widows and single moms, providing haircuts for the homeless, visiting nursing homes and children's homes, and hundreds of other projects. There's nothing like thousands of people in red T-shirts serving all over the city to show the community that God loves them and we love them.

Jesus' Way to Win with People

Jesus gave us the way to win with people: "Do to others as you would have them do to you" (Luke 6:31, NIV). Not only is this good behavior, and honoring to God, but it's also how to win in life and relationships. Be the person you would want someone to be for you. That's the power of kindness. We can do for others what we wish someone would do for us.

How to Win Friends and Influence People, by Dale Carnegie, has sold over 15 million copies and is one of the best-selling books of all time. What I am about to say is in no way intended to take from the wealth of this book. But upon reading it, I put it down and had this simple yet profound thought: *You don't need an exhaustive study of human behavior or a psychologist to decode the secrets to winning with people; you just need to ask yourself, "How would I like to be treated, spoken to, considered?"* And then just *do that* for others. It's pretty simple if we can actually follow it, and that was Carnegie's main premise.

I am fascinated by how we can decode the mystery of winning with people by simply asking, *What would I want someone to do for me in this situation?* It's so simple that we miss it. That sentence went by too fast. Let's ask it again: *What would I want someone to do for me right now? How could someone help me? How could someone solve a problem for me?* Chances are, others are facing the same challenges that you are, so go help them with theirs. The challenge is not discovering the right actions to win with people; it's simply acting on them.

Think about the self-talk in your mind constantly playing what we wish people would do or would have done for us. Now let's do that for others. We get to be those kinds of people and do those things for others. Play the self-talk backward and do what it says for someone else.

You see, more often than not we instinctively or by experience know how to connect through kindness. It's fear that keeps us from making those meaningful connections with people. Connectors are a rare breed of people because they have mustered the resolve to do it afraid. That's right. You may be afraid, but you can still do it. In the coming chapters I will give you some very practical tips to help you do it well.

Key Takeaways

- When people visit your church, they do not just feel good; they feel the goodness of God.
- Churches do not intend to come across as unfriendly, but many get a bad reputation because they are unfocused.
- Most often, bad church experiences are simply unmet expectations.
- Staff and volunteers should steward their influence well and politely greet anyone within ten feet.
- The seeds of evangelism are quiet acts of kindness that have resounding effects.
- Kindness builds a bridge of trust that allows for meaningful connection.
- The secret to winning with people is to think about what you would want someone to do for you, and simply do that for others.

Reflection Questions

1. Do others say that your church is friendly?
2. As a church staff member or volunteer, you're a big deal to guests. Do you think you see yourself properly?
3. What can you do for someone else today that you wish they would do for you?

4

TO OPEN DOORS OF OPPORTUNITY

But I will stay on at Ephesus until Pentecost,
because a great door for effective work
has opened to me, and there are many
who oppose me.

1 CORINTHIANS 16:8-9, NIV

When God opens a door for effective work, He usually does it through a person. There are definitely things happening in the spiritual realm that we cannot see, but what we often see is God opening the heart of a person, and then a door of opportunity.

One of my favorite examples of this is a first-century fashion designer named Lydia. Upon Paul's arrival in Philippi, he shared the message of Jesus with Lydia and the Lord opened her heart to receive Jesus as her Savior. Lydia, a businesswoman specializing in luxury cloth, had a nice house and hosted the first Western church. This Philippian church then opened the door for other church plants throughout Macedonia (see Acts 16).

Lydia's life changed with a connection to Paul and vice versa.

Now think about it for yourself. You are always one connection away from a bigger life. I am not just talking about a greater lifestyle but a broader outlook on life. Many times it is another person who presents a new opportunity to you and/or for you. It takes someone with an expanded view to expand our view. It takes someone who's been there to show us the way. It takes someone who knows someone we should know to make the introduction.

> You are always one connection away from a bigger life.

Your door-opening connective influence can create big worlds for people. You have the opportunity to connect people to God, to friends, and to opportunities to use their gifts. They don't see it yet, but when I meet someone, I see their future. I see them growing in God, connected in the church, flourishing in relationships, and finding their purpose. I see them leading Small Groups, having their first kids together, caring for one another through life's challenges, partnering in business, vacationing together, and celebrating life's milestones together. It takes time, but I see it coming. Connectors can see it before anyone else does.

My Great Door of Opportunity: Belmont University

I barely knew her name at the time, but a high school girl named Amanda ended up having one of the greatest impacts on my life.

On a college visit to Belmont University in Nashville, Tennessee, Amanda thought of me. While touring the university, she recalled my interests in the music industry along with my heart for ministry. With those simple acknowledgments, she brought me back a scholarship and enrollment application.

The Madden Scholarship was a four-year full-ride scholarship awarded to a future pastor to study theology at Belmont University. For someone with no college ambitions or academic qualifications, Amanda's gesture was kind, but I thought it was a lost cause. The day before the application was due, I filled it out, only to reaffirm all of my academic inadequacies with the score ranges for GPA, SAT, and ACT all out of my reach. That's right. I didn't even come close to the minimum! A couple of weeks later, a letter arrived informing me of my expectation. I didn't get it.

But that is not the end of the story. A few days before high school graduation, I got an unexpected phone call that went like this: "Hello, this is Dr. Steve Simpler, Dean of the School of Religion at Belmont University. The person we originally awarded the Madden Scholarship to could not accept it. We would like to offer you a four-year full-ride scholarship to Belmont University. There is no expectation that you will have to meet or obligations you will have to fulfill. All you have to do is say yes." Yes!

Dean Simpler told me that he felt a connection when reviewing my application and, regardless of my poor marks, he felt I was the right choice. When I got to Belmont, I walked the campus with tears in my eyes, so grateful to God for how He used these people to give me this opportunity. I graduated from Belmont in 2001, and even went on to graduate school. Thank you, Amanda!

God works through people, and we can be a part of God's work in someone's life. Our destiny is tied to our relationships, and if you are a connector, many of the relationships will be tied to you. God has gifted you to see people uniquely and introduce them to what may be a destiny-defining opportunity.

Open Doors Through Your Relational World

When you meet someone, they aren't just connecting to you but potentially with everyone connected to you. What greater value to share with someone than a world of relationships? Your greatest gift to someone may not be you but who you know. Who you know and what you know about them are incredibly valuable when making significant connections for others.

I am sure you have heard of the concept of "six degrees of separation." The idea came from an experiment psychologist Stanley Miligram conducted in the 1960s. The study started with 160 individuals in Omaha, Nebraska, receiving a packet. Their instructions were to get the packet to a certain name and address in Sharon, Massachusetts, by using their relational network to do it as efficiently as possible and recording the stops along the way. Most of the letters reached the intended recipient within five or six steps.

A fascinating finding came out of this study, uncovered by Malcom Gladwell in his best seller *The Tipping Point*:

> Yet in the end, when all of those separate and idiosyncratic chains were completed, half of those letters ended up in the hands of Jacobs, Jones, and Brown. Six degrees of separation doesn't mean that everyone is linked to everyone else in just six steps. It means that a very small number of people are linked to everyone else in a few steps, and the rest of us are linked to the world through those special few.[11]

When you choose to be a connector, you can be like one of those Jacobs, Jones, and Browns, where that valuable relational equity links back to you. That is some incredible influence to steward to make our world, our churches, and the worlds of others better.

When you meet someone for the first time, your walk-away thought should often be, *Who do I know who they should know?* Other ways to think through it are: Who would they flow with? Who could they learn from? Who could help them, or who could they help? Who do they remind me of—similar age, interests, style? Who's in a similar season of life, career, family?

Off the top of your head, you can probably answer those questions and narrow them down to a few specific people. This is an example of your relational knowledge—the knowledge you hold of who you know and what you know about them.

Here's how it works practically: The longer you are at your church, the more people you are going to know and the more you'll know about them. Over time and with some intentionality, you learn what they do, where they're from, their interests, family, etc. You also learn their personality. You see how they relate to you and others. You may even see how they steward responsibilities and other relationships in the church. You learn who you can trust and who you can trust others with. You learn who is going to follow through and who lets it fall through.

You may not think about it this way, but you are building an internal database of information regarding the people in your church. It's your relational knowledge database and it's a huge value to the church. You can answer the greatest question of "Who?" Who should lead this team? Start this Small Group? Who can sing? Teach kids the Bible? Who's good at social media? Who has an expertise in writing? Who can do graphics?

Not only is it a value to your church, but it is also a value to the newest people coming into your church. With access to your mental database, you can fast-track their relational life. You already know who they should know. You know who they will and won't flow with.

It took you awhile to learn all those things about those people and all they need to know is *you*. With just one interaction, you can connect them to who they would best flow with and relate to. You know who they live near and you know who has kids their own kids' ages. You know who's faced a similar challenge and can walk with them and pray with them through it. Here are some thought starters:

- Who do I know that they should know? (add relational value)

- Who do they remind me of? (similar season, interests, and affinities)

- Who can help them? (solve the problem, similar testimony)

- Who can they help? (serve others, be a solution)

To feel confident in making these connections for people, you need to have influence. Influence is gained by serving people. The more people you can serve, the more influence you will have.

Open Doors Through Your Relational Influence

Relational influence is the capital you have with others to secure connections. By "secure" I mean this: When you recommend someone to meet someone else, they actually do it. They are eager to do it. When you introduce someone to someone else, they pick up the connection with intentionality. When you ask someone to follow up with someone else, they do it enthusiastically. They know that if *you* are asking them, then it must be worth it.

Influence is one of those things that just takes time to get. I could tell you that "leadership is influence" and you may say, "That's nice," but if John Maxwell said, "Leadership is influence," you would grab a pen and write it down (as I and countless others have, again and again, every time he says it). He has incredible influence in leadership circles because of his incredible insight and the people he's helped. You gain more influence with every person you help.

This influence grows when people feel like you understand them and what they want, and when they perceive that you genuinely want to help them. When someone coming into your church trusts that you care about them and want to help them solve some of their problems, you gain influence.

The first problem to solve for someone new is their "un-known-ness." You have to get to know them—their name, their story, their needs, and their gifts. I remember hearing a story about a young Elvis Presley visiting a church for the first time. He mentioned to someone that he could play the piano. They told him, "We already have a piano player." Elvis never returned. I do not know if this story is true or not, but nonetheless it made its point. Every person is a gift and has a gift, and we need to get to know them to help identify these and to serve them.

I mentioned in the introduction that, even as a kid, I was so impacted when our geographically and relationally disjointed family of six would show up at a church Welcome Kiosk and put our lives in the hands of the volunteer on deck. These amazing volunteers would walk us to Sunday school classrooms, introduce us to teachers, and ease our nerves with chit-chat along the way.

In the coming weeks, these volunteers were the ones who re-membered me, knew my story, and high-fived me in the hall. That was a big deal for me in those seasons of transition. They became my heroes, and so much of their impact has impacted what I still do to this day.

The second benefit of building relational influence is being able to connect people to others with confidence. When you have influence with people, you can make an introduction and know it will stick. You can have peace knowing they won't drop the ball.

—

Connecting people is like a proper pairing of magnets. It's my favorite visual metaphor when connecting people and why I used magnet stones on the book cover art. Practically, magnets get quick to the question "Will they click?" And spiritually, they remind me of "living stones, being built into a spiritual house" (see 1 Peter 2:5). Magnets active with magnetite need the right polarization in order to click, and stones are not randomly stacked but are intentionally placed together.

> Connecting people is like a proper pairing of magnets.

With consideration and intentionality, we can help place people where relationships come together effortlessly. Like magnets, if it is the right polarization, then all you have to do is get them remotely close and they connect themselves. However, if you try to force something that is not there, you'll sense the resistance and will lose some credibility.

The more successful you are at helping people find people they click with, the more influence you will have and the easier future connections will be. People begin to trust that the people you introduce them to are carefully considered and intentionally recommended. They take you at your word when you say, "You'll like them. They'll be great for your team" or "They're a great fit."

> Your responsibility as a connector in your environment is not to be everyone's friend but to help everyone find a friend.

You need to be great at these connections because they can't all click to you. Your responsibility as a connector in your environment is not to be everyone's friend but to help everyone find a friend. You don't have the relational margin to connect everyone to you—you'd no longer be free to connect. You can help a great number of individuals find rich friendships while continuing to build your own.

In simple terms, connectors are like Kingdom matchmakers running through a mental database of people with compatibility factors and matching people to Jesus, to relationships, and to opportunities for them to use their gifts. You have a powerful opportunity to be used by God to bring people together to carry out the purposes God has for them.

Key Takeaways

- You are always one connection away from a bigger life.
- Who you know and what you know about them are incredibly valuable when making significant connections for others.
- When you meet someone for the first time, your walk-away thought should often be, *Who do I know who they should know?*
- Relational influence is the capital you have with others to secure connections.
- Connecting people is like a proper pairing of magnets.
- Your responsibility as a connector in your environment is not to be everyone's friend but to help everyone find a friend.

Reflection Questions

1. Who introduced you to Jesus? Who introduced you to your spouse?
2. Do you see yourself as a relational door opener for people?
3. How could you get better at helping people connect to the right people and opportunities to use their gifts in the church?

5

TO REACH THE COMMUNITY

Philip found Nathanael and told him,
"We have found the one Moses wrote about in
the Law, and about whom the prophets also
wrote—Jesus of Nazareth, the son of Joseph."
"Nazareth! Can anything good come
from there?" Nathanael asked.
"Come and see," said Philip.

JOHN 1:45-46, NIV

Connectors not only bring the world together, but they also bring Jesus to the world. Connectors are the catalyst to reaching your community. They are the one's saying, "Come and see." They aren't just a great gift *in* the church; they connect the community *to* the church. They love their neighbors, they love their church, and they love bringing the two together.

If you think about it, you can probably identify some of these missional connectors in your church who are already living this way. If you were to ask around, "Who invited you? Who brought so-and-so? How did you hear about our church?" you would probably find some common threads linking back to the names of these missional connectors. You may even be shocked to find out who the quiet influencers are. Everyone can do this if they are thinking about connecting the community.

No matter who we meet, we should be thinking, *Man, they'd love my church and love my Jesus!* You can do this because you are confident in your church and the consistent environment it creates for people to encounter Jesus. You know that if you can just get them to show up, their lives could be forever changed. Just as Philip said to Nathanael, all you need to say is "Come and see"— and amazingly, people do time and time again.

Everyone Can Be on Mission

We can all get better at being missional connectors who build spiritual bridges to our communities. Everyone can do this in their own unique way. I especially love helping those who don't feel so extrovertly inclined grow in their confidence to live a life on mission.

Practically speaking, I've found that most people aren't entirely confident to present the gospel, but they are more comfortable inviting someone to church, a church event, or even a Small Group. At Milestone, we have discovered that the vast majority of people who come to faith in Christ in one of our services were there because they were personally invited by someone. Let's encourage and celebrate that.

Some people get uncomfortable with the idea of "invite evangelism," but I don't get it. Why would we not be proud to invite someone to our churches? As my pastor often says, "The best way to know if you are in a healthy church is to ask, 'Would I invite my friends and family?'" I think invite evangelism is one of the best people-reaching strategies on the planet when there is an accessible strong local church.

Please hear me out on this: Going to church won't save you any more than visiting a doctor will make you well, but you are definitely moving in the right direction and in the place for help. Not only is the right medicine prescribed, but

> Connectors not only bring the world together, but they also bring Jesus to the world.

also there are living testimonials all over the place encouraging next steps. What if they keep coming back, week after week? It's just a matter of time before they find their healing. At some point, in a Small Group, in a service, or over coffee with someone they've connected with, our prayer is that the person taking steps makes the ultimate leap to trust Jesus as their Savior.

One of the most clarifying illustrations of this came from my seminary professor Dr. Roy Fish. He told the story of a person drowning in water with a friend treading right by their side. The friend is coaching them to breathe and to keep their head above water, saying, "Watch how I do it! Kick harder! Use your arms!" but never thinking to throw them the life ring. The life ring is the gospel. The gospel is what saves, not church or relationships. They need Jesus, and someone needs to make sure they hear the gospel.

In the book *Transformational Church*, Ed Stetzer and Thom

Rainer (with extensive research) did a nice job of bringing these two together:

> As our culture becomes increasingly less churched, (or interested in church), we are forced to move our methods further back in history to a more ancient approach to reaching people. Some call this transition from *come and see* evangelist church to a post-Christendom *go and tell* missionary church. That is not to say "come and see" is over. It's not. But we need more "go and tell."[12]

I think the answer is right in the middle—we need to do all of it. We create environments people are drawn to, we go out and we invite them in, and we also go out and share the gospel as the Holy Spirit leads us.

You can create a missional-living, community-connecting culture where it is not just expected of a few but also encouraged by all. Things get catalytic when this becomes part of the culture in your church. The Great Commission calls people living their everyday lives to actively engage in a greater mission: "Therefore go and make disciples of all nations, baptizing them in the name of the Father and of the Son and of the Holy Spirit" (Matthew 28:19, NIV).

That is our mission, together with Jesus, to see everyone around us come to know Him personally and follow Him. Once you become a disciple of Jesus, there is no greater purpose than partnering with Jesus to see His Kingdom built. Our hearts begin to beat for what His heart beats for, and we live for what He gave His life for—people.

That means that wherever we are, we should always be thinking, *What is Jesus doing here? Who is He leading me to serve, encourage, and/or befriend?* Here are a few ways missional people live "differently" and are extremely effective at connecting others to churches and ultimately Jesus.

Connectors Sit in the Stands Differently

Missional connectors may be watching their son, niece, or granddaughter play ball but they are on a mission. When they sit in the stands or bleachers, they are around conversations revealing the pains of life—a strained marriage, a family member's sickness, a tough job situation, etc.

With a little observation, they'll notice the dad at a distance down the way. They hear about the family trying to find some steadiness after a cross-country move. They hear about the challenges of parenting and the need for moral anchors in their kids' lives.

With each conversation they hear, they are looking for how they might be a light. They are intentionally seeking to be a friend, meet a need, and invite them into their life, their Small Group, or their church—all with the purpose of introducing them to their Jesus. They might look like an ordinary parent, grandparent, or coach, but make no mistake, they're different. They're on a mission.

Connectors Go to Work Differently

People pay money, travel around the world, live in horrible conditions, and work tirelessly on mission trips, and most every time they return with the same response: "It was the greatest week of my life." Why is that? I would propose it's because, for that week, they were fully committed to partnering with Jesus and His mission, and there is nothing more fulfilling.

In the same way, I think that our jobs can take on a new level of meaning when they are in conjunction with what Jesus is doing. I encourage people to start by simply praying and asking God what He's doing around them at work—to turn the radio down on their drive in and ask God to drop one name on their heart. Trust that the name He gives you is someone the Holy Spirit is already working on, and begin to pray for them.

As you pray, look for opportunities to encourage them. When you feel comfortable(ish), tell them you pray on the way to work and ask if there is anything specific you can add. They may offer up a request or may deny they have anything to pray about, but either way you just crossed the great divide. You've created a spiritual bridge in the workplace. Now it's just a matter of time before they come to you for help or God creates an opportunity to share your story and invite them to church.

Connectors Neighbor Differently

I personally wish I were better at this. I think the busier you get, the more guarded you get with your home time. More and more the garage door goes up, the car goes in, and the door goes down. Reaching our neighbors may be one of the best mission fields we have. God chose to put us next to these people. I'm sure He knows what He is doing and has a purpose in it.

I've learned that we have to be outside. We play out front rather than in the back. We go to the block parties and do our best to be fun, relatable neighbors, even though I am known as "the pastor." I'm not sure if that's good or bad yet. Every Christmas and Easter, we make it a point to bless our neighbors and invite them to church. It's cool to have so many of our neighbors at church with us now, praying for other neighbors. "Come and see what God has done, his awesome deeds for mankind!" (Psalm 66:5, NIV).

Josh and Bethany's Story

Some friends of ours, Josh and Bethany, opened their home up to host a Small Group my wife and I would lead with them. We had some really great couples in the group, but the couple I was most excited about each week never even came to the group. They were their unchurched neighbors. Josh and Bethany had been praying for them and inviting them to church. They often walked their dogs at the same time our group wrapped up each week (strategically), so we made it a point to connect with them in the driveway.

Fortunately, Brandon and Leslie didn't think we were too crazy and they started visiting our church. After a few weeks, Brandon reached out saying he had a question and would like to meet. I started brainstorming all of the regular questions: "What does non-denominational mean? Can I see the church finances? What does the church do for missions?"

We sat down for lunch and Brandon gave me his big question: "How do I know God? My wife and I want to know God." Internally, I was so excited I was freaking out, but externally, I was trying to play it cool. I said, "Yeah, I can help you with that. Let's finish up lunch and go next door to my office. I'll show you some verses in the Bible and we can pray together." As we finished up, I was praying, *Lord, tarry a little longer. Help him not to choke. Please, Lord, he's going to get saved in 10 minutes.*

We went to my office, at which point he reminded me that his wife wanted to do this too. I said, "That's great! This is what we'll do: I'll walk you through some Bible verses, we'll pray together for you to get saved, and then I'll give you the Bible and the verses so you can go home and pray with your wife."

That is exactly what happened. When I saw Leslie, she told me exactly what happened that afternoon when he got home: "He walked in the doors and I saw it on his face." She said, "You did it without me, didn't you?" She wasn't happy. Brandon, scrambling to recover, said, "But hold on, Pastor Steve said that I could save you!" (Well, it's kind of Jesus who does the saving, but give the guy some grace.)

Brandon, a two-hour-long Christ-follower, got down on his knees with Leslie in their living room. He walked her through some Bible verses and prayed with her to commit her life to Christ. It doesn't matter if you've been a Christian for twenty years or two hours, Jesus does the saving and He's just looking for us to be ready to be used by Him.

Remember, this all started with some neighbors simply being missional connectors.

Key Takeaways

- Connectors not only bring the world together; they bring Jesus to the world.
- Once you become a disciple of Jesus, there is no greater purpose than partnering with Jesus to see His Kingdom built.
- Missional connectors are intentional about inviting people to church.
- The vast majority of people who come to faith in Christ in one of our services were there because they were personally invited by someone.
- You can create a missional-living, community-connecting culture where it is not just expected of a few but also encouraged by all.
- Wherever we are, we should always be thinking, *What is Jesus doing here? Who is He leading me to serve, encourage, and/ or befriend?*
- Missional connectors sit in the stands differently, go to work differently, and neighbor differently.

Reflection Questions

1. How important is it that we intentionally connect to reach the world with the good news of Jesus?
2. How could you get better at inviting people in your world to your church?
3. How does a missional connector go about life differently?

SECTION I

THE POWER OF CONNECTION

WHY connection is the
church-culture game changer

(For Everyone in the Church)

SECTION II

THE PRINCIPLES OF CONNECTION

WHAT you can do to be
a better connector

(For Volunteers & Leadership)

SECTION III

THE PROCESS OF CONNECTION

HOW to build a
connection process

(For Leadership)

THE PRINCIPLES OF CONNECTION

Connectors Go First;
Connectors Know Who to Connect to;
Connectors Know What to Say;
Connectors Know How to Add Value;
Connectors Are Intentional with Leaders

This next section will focus on the practical aspects of connection. I call them principles, but they are simply the key things anyone can do to be a better connector.

My focus in this section is connecting with people in the local church and for the mission of Jesus, but these principles can be applied anywhere.

6

CONNECTORS GO FIRST

"Go, stand in the temple courts," he said,
"and tell the people all about this new life."

ACTS 5:20, NIV

I love the instructions of the angel of the Lord in Acts 5: "Go and tell them about this new life." Don't wait for them to come to you. You go to them. This message is too good to keep to ourselves. We need to make the first move to initiate relationships in the world we are reaching. There are lost and lonely people on the fringes of our lives just waiting for us to make the first move.

When I think about going first, I am reminded of a viral campaign that caught my ear some years back called "Be the first to smile." The idea is that when you catch yourself in a stare with another set of eyes, you have the choice to look away, smile first, or smile back. Be the first to smile!

I love this idea because it is such a great experiment to push past our insecurities, our fear of rejection, and make a connection with another person. That person is just like you, going through

69

this life with the same basic need of being known. They are wanting to know if the person on the other end of that gaze accepts them.

When it comes to connection, the scenario is quite similar to smiling at a stranger. In a room full of people, you have the option to wait for someone to engage with you or to courageously choose to engage them. Be the first to connect. Be the first to introduce yourself to the person sitting beside you in church or standing beside you in the kids' pick-up line. Be the initiator. Connectors go first.

It sounds easy, but the thought of that will test your nerves. We start to wonder, *What happens when I put myself out there? What if I'm rejected? What if they get the wrong idea? What if I come across as annoying?* Nobody wants to be the person holding up a line when everyone's in a hurry, or worse, the guy at the gym striking up a conversation in the middle of your set.

I get it. But you shouldn't be concerned if you're already thinking this. You have a social awareness that subconsciously guides you in this world of connection. The person you are thinking of . . . well, they don't have that social awareness, and they aren't thinking about *not* being that person because they *are* that person!

Overcome Fear of Rejection

After training hundreds of people in this area, I would say the primary reason people are hesitant to connect is fear of rejection. They are afraid they might put out the hand or offer up the "Hello, my name is..." only to be met with rejection.

You don't quickly forget the anxiety you feel from a *connection fail*. You put yourself out there and the energy is not reciprocated, the person's responses are short and blunt, and your eyes are scrambling for any escape from the flailing interaction. "Okay, good talk." You walk away with this self-talk playing in your head and it's usually, *What's wrong with me?* or *What's wrong with them?*

It happens. To become a great connector, you must learn how to process a little rejection and not let it sideline you. Accept the fact that not every interaction is going to be great and that some may be a real bust. Some of my biggest busts are now my biggest laughs. (Sometimes you have to laugh to keep from crying.)

Even before I was a pastor, I had a massive failure. During the meet-and-greet of a service, I turned to say hello to the person beside me. I said my name and then he said his quietly, so I asked, "Garret?" To which he said, "No, it's..." and he said something again. I wanted to get it right, so I said, "Jarret?" He said, "No,..." I guessed something else and he just frustratingly said, "Sure."

After the service was over, some of my buddies were excited to see if I got to connect with "Derrick," the NFL Pro-Bowl receiver I was sitting next to. "Uh . . . kind of?" Connection fail! (Although, I did probably settle his nerves about being overly noticed in service.)

> The primary reason people are hesitant to connect is fear of rejection.

Not too long ago I met a really nice couple before service. At the same time, one of my longtime friends and fellow team member was walking by, so I took the opportunity to make sure to connect them as well. I said, "Pastor Eddie, come over here. Have you had the chance to meet the Smiths yet?" Pastor Eddie, without missing a beat, confidently said, "No, I haven't. Nice to meet you," and put out his hand. Unfortunately, the sweet lady, with a little defeat on her face, commented, "You baptized me." Another connection fail!

Another one of my favorite connection fails happened with another one of our pastors, my friend Ron. During the meet-and-greet portion of the church service, he turned around to confidently introduce his wife to a couple he had met the week prior. "Jonathan, Leslie, great to see you guys again. I want you to meet my wife..." They shook hands quickly and turned to sit as the service sharply transitioned to a video. As they found their seats, Ron's wife, a little belligerent, said, "What are you doing? Their names are Charlie and Paige." Whoops, names can be tricky.

I've had so many failures. I've walked away from conversations wondering, *Did I upset them? Was it something I said? Why did I say that?* But usually with these connections gone wrong, it's nothing to do with us and all of what they have going on in their lives.

People have stuff going on, and we just need to extend grace to them. Often when we are connecting, it's on our turf. We may be relaxed but they may be on-guard and not their best self.

The more secure you are, the more you can let that stuff bounce off you. Security comes first from a personal identity in Christ (who you are) and second by getting some practice (what you do). I am talking about repetition. You've got to keep doing it. Keep putting yourself out there. Be confident in who you are in Christ and obedient to put yourself out there to love and serve others around you.

You will get better and better at how to flow and adapt to the personalities of others. That is something we can control. We cannot control others, but we can control our responses. I constantly have to remind myself that the goal is relationships, not being right or justified.

When you are a connector going first, there are a few things you just have to accept: Some people are not going to like you. Some people don't have the emotional energy for a conversation. Some people are too scared to talk with people they do not know. (And some people, unfortunately, can be rude.) But most people are awesome!

Find Common Ground

Every year, my kids' school has a fall event called "Donuts with Dads." It is helpful because it is one of the few connection gatherings I go to where I am not already carrying some influence in the environment, so I get a more honest evaluation.

The first several years I did my usual thing. I was connecting this guy with that guy, pulling people into huddles of men, and making introductions. I was managing the walk-by interactions with cordial eye contact and head nods, bouncing from conversation to conversation, pulling new guys and outsiders in as they came near—typical Donuts with Dads.

But for the last couple of years, I have been experimenting with something. Instead of living "connectors go first," I decided to not "go" at all. I thought, *I am not going to initiate any new interactions and just see what happens. I want to see who else will go first.* I wondered what the other men would do.

What I found is that the only people who engaged with me were people I already knew. Our kids played on the same team or were in the same class, or we knew each other from church. They were men I'd met before. We already had some common ground. No one new introduced themselves to me out of the hundred-plus dads in attendance.

This made me realize how important a common reference point is to connection; we are most comfortable when we already know we share something in common. As long as we are strangers, it feels strange, but as soon as we share something, we form a bond.

That's why so many conversations for men start with, "Cool car, nice watch, Cowboy's fan?" Or ladies often, "I like your hair, nice bag, cute shoes." What we are saying is, "What you like, I like. So there is a chance we may be alike, and we like that." That's why connections around hobbies and interests are much easier for people.

When we don't naturally see the common reference point, we avoid the interaction altogether. But sometimes we are forced to interact. It is in these situations with no apparent common language that we start talking about the weather. "Looks like a cold front is supposed to come through this weekend. . . . Yep, about time. . . . I know, right?" What this means is, I've exhausted my options and all I can think that we share in common is the temperature.

A connector is the first to bring people together by establishing a bridge of commonality before others realize it. These bridges make ground for the dialogue and that's what helps us get to know someone. It's the common ground. It's not easy getting people to be comfortable in conversation. We need something to talk about.

Even if you don't find an immediate common interest, you can look to connect based on their interest if one presents itself. A real art to intentional connection is valuing what they are interested in, not simply finding your common interests. We are ultimately interested in them. Everything else is just a conversation starter.

When you get them talking about what they are passionate about, it's going to be a great connection. When someone gets comfortable talking to you about themselves and what they are passionate about, they walk away thinking how much they like you.

Make Your Move;
Anyone Can Connect

Anyone can be the first to connect. I know that if you're an introvert, you may be thinking you can't be a great connector because you may not be as outgoing. That's not true. Great connectors are great listeners, not just great talkers.

I am an introvert myself. I recharge alone, enjoy time alone, and often find myself wanting to withdraw in large social settings. But I also love people and have a deep desire to reach people for Jesus and connect them in the church. I'm sure you share that desire, so I let's push ourselves out there and start the conversation.

> Great connectors are great listeners, not just great talkers.

And honestly, maybe like you, I sometimes struggle to find the words to keep the conversations going smoothly. And when I do have the words, I can feel when I have been talking for a stretch and the focus has been toward me too long, and that makes me uncomfortable too. The good news is, we can always take the conversational pressure off when we focus on being interested rather than sounding interesting.

Questions are the best way to connect for introverts. I am not talking about an interrogation—nothing controversial, nothing that puts them on the spot or could make them look dumb. Simply help them find something easy and interesting for them to share about. It's helpful and empowering to have a handful of questions at the ready—questions like, "How was your week? How is your family? Did you grow up in this area?"

My favorite ultra-casual question is "How are things?" How open is that? Things? It cracks me up because it is so soft and not at all my personality. It sounds almost like a time-wasting dialogue is about to transpire, but that is the key. That's what I have to remind myself. The goal of the conversation is the building of a relationship, not the topic of discussion.

So, even if you are an introvert, you can be the first to connect.

Key Takeaways

- Connectors go first. We need to make the first move to initiate relationships in the world we are reaching.
- Be the first to introduce yourself to the person sitting beside you in church or standing beside you in the kids' pick-up line.
- Great connectors learn how to process a little rejection and not let it sideline them.
- Great connectors are great listeners, not just great talkers.
- We can take the conversational pressure off when we focus on being interested rather than sounding interesting.

Reflection Questions

1. Are you usually the first to connect, or is someone introducing themselves to you?
2. What do you tell yourself when a connection does not go as well as you had hoped?
3. How could you work to be interested rather than sound interesting in a conversation?

7

CONNECTORS KNOW WHO TO CONNECT TO

From him the whole body, joined and held
together by every supporting ligament,
grows and builds itself up in love,
as each part does its work.

EPHESIANS 4:16, NIV

I've always been intrigued by the "supporting ligament" word choice in Ephesians 4:16. The apostle Paul, inspired by the Holy Spirit, doesn't just focus on the incredible parts of the body but also on the parts that connect them. The Greek word *haphes* translates as "ligament" or "joint." The use of this specific word *haphes* is to call out that even the ligaments are important parts that connect the other important parts so that the whole body can grow.

When you connect in the church, God uses you to be the vital ligament that brings the parts of the body together to grow and build itself up in love. That's a huge contribution. I hope you are stirred like me to do it even more intentionally. But you may be asking, "Who do I connect with?" You are not alone in asking. In fact, this is the question I probably get asked the most.

I love the question "Who do I connect with?" because I know that it is most likely asked with a bias for new people coming into our church environments. I like that spotting the first-time guest is what these individuals—and possibly even you—are thinking about. I will talk about that later in this chapter, but I want to first expand your idea of connection in the church.

Connection is not just new people feeling welcomed but a culture of connection where old and new get connected and stay connected. It's the whole body. When you think about who, it's not just new but everyone. It would be difficult if your only opportunity to feel welcomed and engaged was your first weekend at a church and from then on you had to fend for yourself. That just doesn't make sense.

We don't do it intentionally, but I do think that only focusing on the guests overlooks the greater principle of connection. A connected church is the whole church connected. So let's talk about who to connect to.

Those You Don't Know

The starting point of "Who do I connect to?" would be those you are not yet connected to. This may not be deep theological insight, but think about it some more. Maybe you see someone each week and smile but don't know their name. You're grateful they brew the coffee each week, but you don't know what they do for a living. You see the family that looks a lot like yours but haven't yet invited them to your Small Group. Remember, it's not just connecting to guests but creating a culture of connection.

I know it gets awkward when you know you "should" know someone better than you do. Or you should know their name but you don't. This passive relational engagement reminds me of my interaction with some identical twins I "knew" in college. I always felt bad whenever I saw one of them because I never knew which twin was which. I just determined to give each one an equally shallow greeting rather than really learn who they were.

> Connection is not just new people feeling welcomed but a culture of connection where old and new get connected and stay connected.

I think we can get caught in a similar trap in our churches just seeing people week to week but not really knowing them. Let's figure out a way to reconnect and get to know them and not just see them. Maybe this weekend you can stop and have a conversation with the person sitting beside you before you exit the worship center. Tell them how the message spoke to you and what challenged you personally. (Yeah, that just got vulnerable.) You'll be surprised when they reciprocate.

Connectors set a cultural tone for this type of engagement. They are the ones doing it so others can model after them. What an amazing place when everyone is looking to know and be known by those around them. Every new interaction is an opportunity to help each other take spiritual steps.

When a church grabs ahold of this, it turns a gathering of believers into a family of believers. Everyone begins to be aware of each other's needs and help each other where they are gifted. The more people know each other, the more opportunity for cross connections to help serve one another and build up the body.

Those Who Intimidate You

Connect with the person who intimidates you. I have found this to be the best way to say it, and it answers the key question every time. Again, the question I get over and over again from church leader after church leader is "Who do I connect with?" Answer: Start with the person who intimidates you.

When everyone connects with the person who intimidates them, I am convinced we can connect with everyone. When we connect only with people who we are comfortable with, what we are doing is connecting with people we already know or people we tend to think we are *better than*. Sorry, there's no easier way to put it. Unfortunately, when we compare ourselves to others, we feel confident when we feel superior but intimidated when we feel inferior. We'd much rather feel confident, so we often avoid those who intimidate us.

My friend John made this so obvious to me one night as we were having dinner together. He was telling me that he had finally connected with a new gentleman in the church I had asked him to reach out to. It had been several weeks since I had asked, and just the week prior I had asked him if he had connected with him, and he had apologetically said no. In fact, he told me he was a little intimidated to reach out and that was the delay. I told him, "You can't be intimidated. If you're intimidated, then there's no one else I can think of to connect to this gentleman."

So, as we sat at dinner, he caught me up on the connection. He reached out to this individual to grab coffee and as they talked, it was like they were living the same life: same age, same industry, same management level, and kids the same age. I said, "I know! That's why I wanted you to connect with him, but you were scared to talk to *you*."

You'd probably be intimidated by you. Seriously, if you walked into a room, you'd think you are a pretty big deal. It's hard to see ourselves accurately, but the best way to relate to others is to remember that they aren't thinking about you; they are thinking about themselves and their own insecurities. They are walking away thinking about what you thought of them and the cheesy thing they said.

Whatever environment you find yourself in, look around, find someone who intimidates you, and make your move. It may be at a Small Group, a weekend service, or a community activity. Let the nerves be a clue you are engaging the right person. Lean into the fear rather than run from it. There is a potential relationship and opportunity for ministry at stake.

*Fear of man will prove to be a snare, but whoever
trasts in the Lord is kept safe.*

PROVERBS 29:25, NIV

There is too much at stake to let intimidation limit your connection to people, especially the people who God sends in the doors of our churches. We cannot allow fear of man, comparison, or whatever the snare may be to keep us from following the Holy Spirit's leading to connect to someone.

I've found that when churches fail to do this, they are not able to keep sharp leaders. When leaders visit a church for a service or an activity, and people do not engage with them because of intimidation, they do not feel welcomed. Leaders must connect with leaders.

> People get excited for the one but forget there are ninety-nine you have to leave to go after the one.

When surveying people's experiences visiting churches, I have found it is the sharp leaders who don't self-initiate who get missed; it is the self-assured person who walks with determination, even if they do not know where they are going; it is the standoffish person evaluating the environment before they open up relationally. If I ever talk to someone who did not get engaged at an earlier visit, it is usually this profile.

These are the people I am on the lookout for—the ones who might get missed but have incredible promise. Keep things cool, don't press, but serve them at the point of their need. You're usually a few answered questions away from them opening up.

Go After the One

We have limited time, limited energy, and limited opportunities to connect with people on the weekend at church, so it needs to be intentional. We get pulled in all different relational directions and responsibilities, but as a connector our highest priority should be the unconnected. They are the ones coming into our environment new, unknown, and most impressionable.

Our time to spot these individuals in the crowd is limited. We have a chance to connect before a service, briefly in a meet-and-greet, and maybe after service before they dash off. So, when we add it up, we really only have a few minutes before service, a thirty-second meet-and-greet, and maybe ten minutes as they linger outside—about fifteen minutes to look for the one. It's reminders like this email that encourage me to keep focused on the one.

FROM: JAN
SUBJECT: THANK YOU!
TO: INFO@MILESTONECHURCH.COM

Good morning!

My name is Jan and I attended Saturday night service last night with my boyfriend and daughter. After the wonderful message Pastor Steve walked up behind us and introduced himself to my boyfriend, John. I've been a member at Milestone for about 2 years now and attend on a regular basis. John on the other hand works weekends and has only attended maybe 2 services with me. I wanted to thank Pastor Steve for weaving through the crowd to talk to him. I feel as though it was such a God thing. He has had a horrible couple of weeks. For him to take 2 seconds to talk to us after service to show that Milestone is loving and caring and recognizes an unfamiliar face in the crowd makes my heart so happy. John knows how much I love Milestone and for him to receive a warm welcome from this pastor is the cherry on top! Thank you to all the staff at Milestone for being so awesome and especially Pastor Steve for simply introducing himself!

Many blessings,

Jan

In Luke 15, Jesus tells the story of a shepherd who leaves ninety-nine sheep and goes after the one that is lost. There are lost sheep in every church service. Some are lost spiritually and some are lost relationally. If you ask the Holy Spirit to help you, He will lead you to the one.

People get excited for the one but forget there are ninety-nine you have to leave to go after the one. I want to talk about identifying the one, but let's first identify the ninety-nine you will often have to leave behind for a little bit: *friends, favorites,* and *familiars.*

The church is a gathering of awesome people. Many of your best *friends* on the planet are all together in one spot once a week. If you're on a church staff, these are some of your coworkers, or maybe you're a key volunteer and those you serve beside are your closest friends. They are the "ninety-nine." It's so hard but these are conversations you have to avoid as you stay focused on the one.

The next group of ninety-nine, distracting from the one, are some of your church *favorites*. These are people who, when you see them, you genuinely light up. Maybe they're a rockstar volunteer, a person you led to Christ, or someone you've been in Small Group with. These people make local church ministry great. But this group may or may not be focused on the one yet. What you need to do here is help them see what you see. Help them be part of looking for the one and do it together. When you look together, they will not feel like you are looking past them.

Finally, a broad group you'll have to leave to find the one is the *familiars*. These are people who know you, who feel comfortable with you, and who would have no problem talking to you for an hour. They're not friends; they're not favorites; they are good people who love proximity to you but are not as focused as you on the mission. They have time to talk because they aren't contributing in the search for the one. Show kindness and acknowledge these individuals, but keep moving. Don't get stopped. Stay on the search for the one.

To connect with people, you have to be free. I think this is one of the hardest things to do, especially if you are a relational person. It feels super vulnerable, standing by yourself, or moving casually about, waiting on a great connection opportunity. We would much rather be in a stationary conversation or march around with determined direction. But remember, you are on a mission to connect, not just to converse.

We stay free by not getting wrapped up in distracting conversations during these small windows of connection. I talked about leaving the ninety-nine and going after the one—many times that search involves only you. You have to get comfortable moving on your own, staying free, and being available to connect.

I suggest positioning yourself in an area where the flow of people comes to you. This may be at an entrance to the building, a worship center, a children's building, or classroom door—somewhere where people are coming to you and you are not having to chase people down. As people move by you, greet and acknowledge them, and when someone stands out, engage in conversation. (We'll talk about how to do this and what to say in the next chapter.)

Steward Your Time and Influence

It's hard to bypass familiar dialogues and focus on new connections. Often, these are people you really like; but remember, what you are doing is too important to not be focused. So how do you stay focused on guests without creating offense with those you may have to pass by as you stay free to connect?

It is such a delicate balance to be cordial to everyone and stay available for the one. I have learned by trial and error and am still growing in this. There was a season when I was so focused that I created a lot of offenses. There began to be whispers: "Pastor Steve used to be my friend" or "Pastor Steve only has time for the new people now." Ouch, that still hurts.

The truth is, with our church's rapid growth, any time on the weekends was focused on the new people, but I needed to figure out how to still add value to new and old alike. During this season I made some adjustments that really helped. I started to do these three things: set expectations earlier, involve them in the intentionality of what I do, and finally something I call "touch and go." Let me break them down so you can learn from my mistakes and not have to repeat them.

The first adjustment I made was to set expectations earlier. When I connected with someone, my intention was to make sure they found a friend, but their expectation was that we would become friends. It's not that I do not want to be their friend (and many become great friends along the way), but my driving focus is to help them find relationships, not personally fulfill their relational needs. I had to be clearer about this by letting them know my role and how I wanted to help them meet certain people, find a Small Group, and take growth steps. Maybe I can't be their best friend, but I can help them find some friends.

The second adjustment I made happens primarily during weekend services when you are building established relationships while also looking for new people who need to be welcomed. This is when you are engaged in conversation but you don't want it to seem like you are looking over their shoulder or are not interested in them. What I learned to do here is to use those opportunities to focus them on what I am focused on so that we can now do it together. "Have you gotten to meet any new people today?" Or if you see someone, "Do you know that person over there? Let's go say hello."

Finally, the last major personal correction I made was something in my head that I think of as "touch and go." In the past I was guilty of completely and unintentionally ignoring some people while looking for and engaging new people. I would fly right by them and, as you can imagine, hurt some feelings. What I learned to do was acknowledge them briefly in a sincere way but continue to keep moving with purpose. Touch and go. Even so, I am still constantly reminding myself to walk slowly and smile.

Know Who's New

One of the keys to creating a connection culture is a bias toward first-time guests. Everyone matters, every time the doors open, but there needs to be a focus on those coming through the doors for the first time. Your website, parking lot, staff, volunteers, greeters, signage, child check-in, and help desks need to be focused on these three questions: Who's coming here for the first time? Who's new or newer? How can we best serve them above all others? The ability to identify guests is the foundation of a connection culture.

When my wife and I visited Milestone Church on the grand-opening weekend, we stood out. We were the ones who everyone else didn't know. It was pretty simple to know who the guests were at 100 people and even 200 people. At 300 people the key leaders could recognize them. At 500 people the staff could. But with multiple services and compounding weekends, it was getting trickier. Up to 1,000 I believe that a dialed-in staff member should be able to recognize a new face on the weekend. At 1,500 the new face may stand out but it may be their second or third visit. It could also be the family member in town visiting who you met last Easter, or someone who served for a while, left for a bit, but now is back. As the church keeps growing, it gets more complicated, so we must become more intentional.

As the church grows, it is important that the guest self-identification points become more of a focus. Then it is time to focus your connection teams and processes here (guest parking, main-door greeters, child check-in, Guest Central, Guest Suite, reception, Welcome Kiosk, etc.). We will talk about this more extensively in the next section. The key is to create clear opportunities for guests to conveniently identify themselves as guests if they choose to do so.

A subtle thing I've found is that guests are often early to their seats in the worship center and they are the only ones reading the screen or bulletin/brochure. If you walk up to someone reading the brochure and introduce yourself, chances are good that they are a guest or pretty new. If not and you don't know them, use it as an opportunity to encourage them and help them with their next step of engagement.

Look Out for Dynamic Transfers

Every weekend there is the potential of a seasoned "volunteer rockstar" from another church walking in the front doors of your church for the first time. They know Jesus, have been discipled, have passed the character tests, have led teams, and now they are a first-time guest at your church. I call them "dynamic transfers." If we think Kingdom, God transferred them from one local church to yours for a reason, so lucky you!

I remember when one of my favorite couples was transferred by work to Nashville, Tennessee. This amazing family got saved and discipled in our church, led Small Groups, led teams, gave generously, and connected lots of people from the community. They grew to not only lead but to also lead leaders, and many people just assumed they were on staff because of their ownership of the vision. They were the kind of couple you want all of your guests to meet because you know they would love them and be loved by them.

Soon after they moved to Nashville, I remember thinking, *They are going to walk in the doors of some church in Nashville, and this church has no idea the gift they are about to receive.* A dynamic transfer from Texas just brought a huge lift to their environment, simply by showing up at their church. That prayer Jesus told us to pray in Luke 10, about how the harvest is plentiful but the workers are few, well, these are the workers someone's been praying for. Will that person recognize and utilize them?

I started wondering if I was recognizing and utilizing the dynamic transfers that were coming in our doors. What if a couple like that shows up at our church this weekend? What if there are couples or individuals like that in our services, in our processes now, but not on our radar? Are we serving them uniquely, or do we expect them to follow the same process as someone visiting a church for the first time?

As our team started researching, we found that most people (especially families with school-aged kids) make a move, or transition, over the summer. This makes sense. So why don't we get more intentional about identifying and serving dynamic transfers in the summer? We decided to make it a real focus and help them with their greatest needs and questions.

The greatest needs for dynamic transfers coming into your church are most often getting their kids connected, finding new friends for themselves, and using their gifts.

Connecting Their Kids

For families, the hardest part of a move is how hard it is on the kids. Every parent has a little guilt and is concerned how the move will affect the development of their child. One of the greatest hopes of a parent is for their kids to connect in the children's or student ministry and make solid friendships that will anchor them in their new school.

Student ministry gatherings, camps, mission trips, retreats, pool parties, Small Groups, after-church socials, Vacation Bible School, Sunday school, and service projects are all great environments to make these connections. Make sure your kids and student teams know the individuals and help broker the connections with other kids who they'll flow with and who may be in their school district.

Finding New Friends

These dynamic-transfer adults are looking for friends themselves. The hardest part of the move to your area was saying goodbye to close friends and family. One of the questions they are asking is "Will we have what we had back home?" Part of them feels that trying to build those relationships again is just too exhausting, while another part knows they need to push into the pain of it. They know the importance of community, Small Groups, spiritual family, and doing life together. (Remember, they were probably the leaders of their last group.)

When they come in your doors, they may not be ready to lead just yet, but they want to make sure they have a good leader and are connecting with other leaders. Staff and key leaders need to be aware and help with this matchmaking. People tend to stick where they find a match.

Using Their Gifts

The last big need these dynamic transfers have is to be needed—to use their natural and spiritual gifts. Remember, this individual is already a Christian, so they are not looking to simply consume but contribute. They want to know if this is a church where God would place them to use their gifts to build the Kingdom. I want to be very clear with these individuals that we have a process of vetting, but I also want to validate their prior experience of leading.

94

People will often tell you all they have done, but real leaders will make you draw it out of them. I want to ask enough questions to learn about their years of quiet faithfulness, serving behind the scenes, passing character tests, overcoming offenses, being faithful with little, and being faithful with much. I want to validate their development process so that they know they are known in that sense and I can cast vision for a place of leadership as they take the steps in our process.

Finally, regarding dynamic transfers, and this is a big deal, they need to be protected. Someone with enough influence in the church and with a vision for their long-term impact needs to give them permission to say no to every ask. Because they will be asked a lot. (They are like LeBron James showing up at a pick-up game.) Dynamic transfers attract other dynamic leaders in your organization, and they will all recruit them for their team. I like that, but someone with the influence to do so needs to guide them toward the opportunity that is best for them.

Key Takeaways

- Connection is not just new people feeling welcomed but a culture of connection where old and new get connected and stay connected.
- The most common question is "Who do I connect to?" The answer is simple: people you're not yet connected to, with a focus on new people.
- Connect with the person who intimidates you. When everyone connects with the person who intimidates them, we end up connecting with everyone.
- People get excited for the one but forget there are ninety-nine (the friends, favorites, and familiars) you have to leave to go after the one.
- To avoid any relational offense, focus others on the search for the one with you.
- The ability to identify guests is the foundation of a connection culture.
- Have an intentional process for dynamic transfers (connect their kids, help them find friends, and utilize their gifts).

Reflection Questions

1. Who should you be connecting with at church?
2. What does it mean to leave the ninety-nine and go after the one, in regards to connection?
3. Do you have an intentional plan for connecting dynamic transfers?

8

CONNECTORS KNOW WHAT TO SAY

Greet all God's people in Christ Jesus.
The brothers and sisters
who are with me send greetings.

PHILIPPIANS 4:21, NIV

The second most frequently asked question I get when teaching on connecting people in the local church is this: "When you meet someone new, how do you know what to say?" This is a great question. The answer I am going to give you is so simple, but it has successfully become the go-to conversation opener for so many. I literally say it 10-20 times every weekend. I'll give it to you in just a minute.

But first, let me say, if you have ever asked yourself this question it shows you are a person who cares to engage beyond friendly eye contact and a polite smile. This is a big deal. You are not only going to acknowledge a person standing nearby, but you are also about to use actual words. You are about to communicate your care and concern for someone out loud. That sounds funny to say but that's where most people hit the eject button. They will do anything but talk.

Too many times I've heard the stories of people visiting a church but leaving disappointed because nobody talked to them. That just doesn't make sense to me. We need to talk to them. We can open doors and have some engaging eye contact, but it is not until we talk that we make a meaningful connection.

First Words of Engagement

I want to give you the exact words to break the silence and make the connection. You don't have to be creative and constantly come up with something new. It's like a card up your sleeve you can use at any turn. Here is exactly what I say to every new person I meet at my church:

"Hello, my name is Steve. How long have you been coming to Milestone Church?"

Feel free to take it for yourself and fill in the blanks.

"Hello, my name is _____ . How long have you been coming to _____ Church?"

Change it up if you want, get creative, but this exact phrasing has been tested a thousand times. To be honest, the only difference is that I may change out "hello" for "hey there" or "what's up, guys" depending on the person or couple. Let me break it down for you.

First, with this introductory line, you are staying in a safe assumption zone. You may be meeting a first-time guest to your church or one of the founding members. It doesn't matter; your question works either way. Nobody wants the awkwardness of assuming someone is new only to find out they've been there longer than you. But you also don't want to call out that they've been unnoticed by you up until this point.

Another assumption you avoid with this introduction is volunteering someone's newness to your environment. Even if you know it is someone's first visit, there is no value in calling that out. For starters, you could be wrong and that's not good. But ultimately, when you call out someone's newness it points out that they stand out. It forces them to ask, "What is it about me that's not fitting in here?" They may be brand-new, and that's worth valuing them accordingly, but let them tell you first.

Back to breaking down the introduction. When you introduce yourself, "Hello, my name is...," it welcomes them to volunteer their name without you having to ask. When they tell you their name, make it a point to listen and not just think about your next response. It's a loss when they give you their name and you forget it within a minute because you weren't listening when they told you.

Now, continuing with our introduction: "How long have you been coming to _____ Church?" The individual's response to this question is so valuable because it gives you information to best guide the conversation. There are really only a couple of response options.

First option: If they say we've been coming for some time, then you can say, "Forgive me for not having met you sooner" or "If we've met before, forgive me for not remembering your name." Either way, you are showing value to them now even if you've missed it before. Simply find out where they are involved and discover more about them.

The second option (my favorite) is when they say, "It's our first time," "We're new" or "relatively new" to the church. Perfect! They volunteered it; now you can celebrate it and serve them accordingly.

Follow-Up Question for Understanding

If I learn they are new, in order to best connect them, I want to know two things: how they got here and where they are coming from.

How did they get here?

Do they already have any anchors/relationships in the church? Is church an entirely new experience for them? Did they get invited by a friend, did they drive by, or did they see some marketing? If they already have some friends in the church, I can then partner with the friend to help connect them. If they have no other connections in the church, then that increases the value I can bring to them by helping them find a connection. It also means the connection stakes are higher because there are not any other relational anchors.

Where are they coming from?

I want to know where they are coming from both spiritually and geographically, if church/God/Christianity is a brand-new thing to them, or if they are a committed Christian church leader who has just moved to our area. I want to know if they are coming from another church in our region and if that transition was a good thing. I want to know if this is their first time to walk into the doors of a church.

I have found a simple question that answers those questions and tells me almost everything I want to know about someone who has identified himself or herself as a new person.

"Are you new to the area or just new to _____ Church?"

This question opens the door to a host of information. First, if they are established in the area but new to church in general that tells me this is all unfamiliar to them. This is exciting. How can we help them on this journey of connecting with God? This is what it's all about!

Second, if they are established in the area, new to our church, but coming from another church, they will usually be quick to share this. "We've been at our church for a while, but we've recently started visiting some other churches in the area." Here is where you want to use great discernment to make sure they are following God and not just leaving because of an offense. I have found the most common reason that people make this transition is either for their kids to better connect or they no longer feel confident inviting people to their previous church.

And finally, if they are new to the area, this question allows someone to express their former church engagement, and we want to know this. "We just moved here from _____ and know how important it is for us to find a new church family." They may go on to say that "We were really involved in serving so it feels odd to come in and be the guests." You'll learn about the weight they carried. They possibly led Small Groups, taught classes, or helped oversee a particular ministry in the church.

> People value being heard. People love to talk about themselves and their challenges, so let them.

This is how you can discover who the dynamic transfers are who may have been relocated to your area. These folks are amazing gifts because another church did the work of discipleship and your church now reaps the rewards of a worker.

Listen More; Talk Less

We are talking in this chapter about knowing what to say, but sometimes it's knowing what not to say. When you are getting to know someone, learn about them, serve them, and listen to them, but remember to let the conversation breathe a little.

Not long ago a gentleman requested a phone meeting with me. He wanted to connect with me and get some input on organizational challenges he was facing. I was happy to do it and scheduled a thirty-minute phone call to see how I could help him out.

The meeting came and I took the call in my office, eager to help. Right at the start of the call, I let him know I looked forward to the thirty minutes we had together but, unfortunately, I had a hard stop at half past the hour. The gentleman got right to it and didn't stop for 28 minutes. My assistant and I just exchanged puzzled faces and listened the whole time.

I have no idea what he thought when he hung up the phone. Maybe I was a great help? A great ear? I was perplexed. But it reminded me of how prone we can be to over-talk and under-listen.

People value being heard. People love to talk about themselves and their challenges, so let them. The way to connect with someone is to get them talking about themselves rather than asking about you. People feel most valued when they feel known, and that means they feel heard and understood.

Spacing Says Something

There's more to a conversation than just the words being spoken. Body language is key, but even more important is spacing, or distance. Personally, if I can feel someone's breath or see some spit fly out, then I'm out. When someone moves in too close, I'll back up and start talking louder. If they move in again, I'll change position, put out a foot wedge, and create a false front.

Social awareness in regards to our physical distance is so important when connecting with people. Unfortunately, some people just don't have this awareness, and we can all get better. Just because *we* are comfortable with our spacing doesn't mean *they* are. Nobody wants to have a conversation with a space invader.

There are some cultural and innate expectations on how physically close we should approach someone based on the nature of the relationship and setting. Naturally, the distance is kept greatest with strangers and closest with family, but what is the best distance for a conversation with someone we are connecting with?

Fascinating research done by anthropologist Edward T. Hall determined there were four distinct zones that each come with unspoken rules of engagement. It's important to not violate a zone when connecting with people. They will feel uncomfortable when too close, or we can come across unapproachable if too far. We want to relax people to serve them best, and sometimes that simply comes down to the appropriate distance.[13]

Based on Hall's findings, I put together the following chart to help distinguish these different zones. Note that the best distance for connection is in the social space of four to twelve feet.

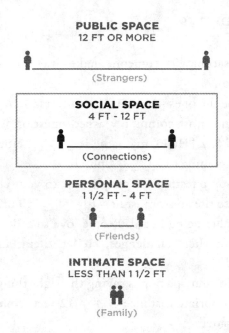

PUBLIC SPACE
12 FT OR MORE

(Strangers)

SOCIAL SPACE
4 FT - 12 FT

(Connections)

PERSONAL SPACE
1 1/2 FT - 4 FT

(Friends)

INTIMATE SPACE
LESS THAN 1 1/2 FT

(Family)

Key Takeaways

- A conversation with someone makes way for a meaningful connection.
- We can be the ones who start the conversation.
- The second most commonly asked question is "What do you say?" Say, "Hello, my name is _____. How long have you been coming to _____ Church?"
- A follow-up question for people new to your church: "Are you new to the area or just new to _____ Church?"
- People value being heard. People love to talk about themselves and their challenges, so let them. Listen more. Talk less.
- Make sure your spacing is saying the right things. Connect at an appropriate distance of 4 to 12 feet. Nobody likes a space invader.

Reflection Questions

1. Are you confident introducing yourself to new people at your church?
2. Do you know what to say when meeting new people at church?
3. How could you become better at listening when someone is sharing?

9

CONNECTORS KNOW
HOW TO ADD VALUE

*And he brought him to Jesus. Jesus looked at
him and said, "You are Simon son of John.
You will be called Cephas"
(which, when translated, is Peter).*

JOHN 1:42, NIV

The greatest value you can add to someone is to really know them, and that starts with knowing their name. Not only did Jesus know Simon's name, but He also saw the potential for who he would become: Peter, "The Rock." When we meet someone, we get the chance to know who they say they are while helping them toward the greater things God has called them to.

Jesus didn't just see Peter as one of the twelve disciples. He saw Peter as one person. Every person is unique, and that is how Jesus sees each of us. In the same way, we should see the potential of each individual. As connectors we must first ascribe value to the person before we can add value to the person.

The greatest way to show someone they are more than a number and more than a face in the crowd is to simply know their name. No matter how big your church is, when someone is greeted by name, it feels like home. It feels like they belong.

There are a lot of things we can get right (and potentially wrong). Hopefully, people will follow God's leading, but I have found people often feel led to stay where they feel valued, wanted, and appreciated. There is no better way to communicate value than to remember someone's name.

If someone is greeted by name on their return visit to your church, it's the ultimate value-add—it's a done deal; they're home. They're pretty much family. You're already on a first-name basis!

Marty, a member of our church, said, "I came back to visit the church for the second time and someone walked up and greeted me by name. I was shocked. That's when I knew this was our church home."

Remember People's Names

"How do you remember people's names?" I have been asked this very question hundreds of times from all kinds of people, so this is something you are not alone in. After years of experience and research in this area, I believe I can solve this challenge for you. Name memorization comes down to one thing: motivation.

Our motivation to know someone's name is usually on the wrong side of the introduction. What I mean is, we don't really care to remember their name and who they are until after we've heard their story and made a connection. Since that comes after the introduction, we get caught reflecting on a positive interaction, thinking, *I wish I could remember their name(s).*

The three keys to remembering names are: listen, record, and reference.

Listen

If you want to remember someone's name, you first need to hear it. Often, the problem is that when we introduce ourselves to someone for the first time, we are thinking about what to say next and not what they just said—their name. So the first key is to make it a point to listen when you make the initial introduction.

Once you hear their name, make a point to respond using their name: "Nice to meet you, _____." I don't think there is any memory magic in saying it back to them, but I do think if you have this as a goal, it focuses you to intentionally listen when they say their name.

If during the course of the conversation you happen to forget it, no worries. Before you walk away, simply say, "Forgive me, but what was your name again? I want to make sure I remember you."

Record

Now that you know their name and story, you need to record it somewhere before you forget it. Write it down, or type it in your phone, but find somewhere to record it while it is fresh. Personally, I use the Notes app on my cell phone.

Whenever I walk away from a new connection, I quickly pull out my phone and record some notes. Along with their name I will enter as many supporting details I can recall. This is where memory experts all agree: It is important to attach as many descriptive details to the name as you can. Quirky descriptions and correlations that form mental impressions are the best way to lock in that person's name and face.

Example of notes you would see in my phone:

CONNECT NOTES

DAN: Dan the man, man's man, hunter, tall, brown hair, forties, West Texas, CPA, recommended 101, questions about baptism: 817-###-####.

HAWTHORNE FAM: Dave and Julie, moved from CA, 2 kids, middle school, invited by neighbors, the Bakers, help get kids connected to student ministry.

It looks random, but those details paint a picture and remind me how I can best serve these people. The more details I put, the better I'll be at remembering their names, their story, and really connecting them at our church. I constantly discipline myself to record more than I think I will need to remember, because if not, I forget.

Reference

The final tool to remembering names is the ability to reference. With the name in your Notes app or written somewhere convenient, you can now go back and reference it anytime. The best time is the next time you see them and you are scrambling to recall their name. Simply reference your notes and greet them by name—that's it. After a weekend of church services, I will go back and review my notes to see the names of people I met and see if there is a way I might serve them in the week ahead.

> No matter how big your church is, when someone is greeted by name, it feels like home.

Re-Remembering Names Takes Humility

Remembering names of returning guests is huge, but so is remembering the names of regular church attenders—re-remembering the names you once knew but have now forgotten. You want to avoid the situation where you are dodging someone simply because you should know their name but don't. This is where humility comes in.

Sometimes a familiar person comes to me for prayer whose name I should know but I cannot remember it at the moment. I get caught in the name-knowing crosshairs. If I ask their name, I'll surely offend them, so I say, "Lord, I pray for this dear brother. Lord, You know him by name, and You see him. He's a dear man, a good man. Encourage my brother in Christ [whose name I do not remember, but You do]. In Jesus' name, amen."

I know we think it may be insulting to ask someone to remind you of their name. However, the greater disrespect is to ignore them rather than mention you need to be reminded of their name. Here's what I say: "Please forgive me, but I am blanking. Can you remind me of your name?" The only disrespectful thing you could do here is to ask them several times without remembering.

In chapter 15, I will share with you how we capture the pictures of each individual who engages our membership process. This is an incredibly helpful tool because you can put a name and a face together. We even print these pictures and keep them on our People Board for one year to help us remember names and help people take steps.

Surprise and Delight Them

Add value by making them really feel something. The Ritz-Carlton has a mantra among their team culture to "surprise and delight" their guests. Team members, whom they refer to as "ladies and gentlemen," are constantly on the lookout for special moments to communicate value to their guests.

They have discovered that surprising and delighting their guests with something outside their expectations really makes them feel cared for. Because the Ritz-Carlton brand already has such a high reputation for excellent service, they have to be that much more creative to exceed it.

In this same way, growing, life-giving local churches have a high bar of expectation already to meet. When you share with someone that you'll be praying for them, that is expected. However, when you follow up a few days later for a status update, that will surprise and delight them. It seems small, but a moment that anchors one's heart to the church is the difference between saying you care and showing you care.

These opportunities are everywhere. They usually require an extra step, but they communicate that you really value people. It goes beyond the requirements of a job, volunteer role, or even an expectation of a Christian.

These extra steps stand out as a genuine act of love and concern for someone. We often feel it, and we know they matter greatly to God; we just need to look for opportunities like these to communicate it. Then they will feel it too.

Serving Is the Greatest Way to Add Value

Jesus spoke some of the most revolutionary words to ever enter our vernacular when He said that the "greatest among you will be your servant" (Matthew 23:11, NIV). Completely flipping the hierarchy of societal importance, He gave us the secret to gaining influence with people—serve them; put them first.

Jesus understood that the only way that love comes out of our heart and into another's is through serving. When we serve people, they feel loved, and we gain influence with them. Jesus not only spoke those words, but He also lived those words all the way to the cross to communicate His love for us.

Serving is the greatest way to love others and add value to their lives. I love this excerpt from one of my favorite messages ever preached and one of Dr. Martin Luther King's final messages, "The Drum Major Instinct." It beautifully communicates how all of us, by choosing to serve, can greatly add value to others.

> And so Jesus gave us a new norm of greatness. If you want to be important—wonderful. If you want to be recognized— wonderful. If you want to be great—wonderful. But recognize that he who is greatest among you shall be your servant. [Amen] That's a new definition of greatness.

> And this morning, the thing that I like about it: by giving that definition of greatness, it means that everybody can be great, because everybody can serve. You don't have to have a college degree to serve. You don't have to make your subject and your verb agree to serve. You don't have to know about Plato and Aristotle to serve. You don't have to know Einstein's theory of relativity to serve. You don't have to know the second theory of thermodynamics in physics to serve. You only need a heart full of grace, a soul generated by love. And you can be that servant.[14]

Make as Many Promises as You Can Keep

Whenever I engage with someone at church on the weekend, my leading thoughts are to make as many promises as I can keep—promises that will serve this individual or family in a special, customized way. This may be a promise to pray for them, get them information they are requesting, connect them with someone, answer a question, or sign them up for an event.

It doesn't matter how small the need may be; you can make a huge impact by helping them meet it. They could probably do it themselves just as easily, and maybe even quicker, but that doesn't matter. We want to do it for them because it is an opportunity to communicate value. We know that the solution to their need(s) may be obvious on our website or solved easily by calling the church office, but we are in the people-serving business and should jump at the chance to serve them.

Show them you are willing to go the extra mile and send them the link directly or sign them up for the event yourself. Tell them you'll have the appropriate ministry leader follow up with their need or concern. Work with the team to ensure someone calls them with the solution before they can call with the question.

When we interact with someone on the weekend at one of our services, any conversation can easily present an opportunity to serve them in a special way that communicates God's value for them. Think about how you would treat your most valuable member and treat everyone with this value. In the same way you would go out of your way for them, go just as far for everyone you can.

But as I said, only make as many promises as you can keep. You have to employ a deliberate note-taking strategy to ensure you deliver on your word. Just as great a positive value you can make with your follow-through, you can make as negative of an impression with failure to follow through.

Personally Follow Up

Everyone expects you to be nice and excited to meet them on Sunday, but what really communicates value is when you follow up with the same excitement on Monday. One of my favorite things to do to show we really value the people we connect with on the weekend is following up with those individuals we personally meet.

This is not the follow-up process that goes to everybody but a personalized follow-up to key individuals you had meaningful interaction with. We have a follow-up process that includes an email (the info) and a handwritten card we mail with a gift card (the "wow"), which we send to everybody. I will cover this in the next section, the Process of Connection.

This extra email, text, or phone-call follow-up is a lifeline out to your weekend connection that catches them in the stride of their week and natural life rhythms. It bridges the gap between the church world and their world and communicates care and concern for them. Everyone expects you to be nice in church, but this shows that you really are nice.

This follow-up could come from a team member or a church member; either way, the impact is equally great. Here is a sample of something I might say through email or text:

> So great to meet you last weekend. If there is anything I can do to serve you and your family, don't hesitate to let me know. Also, if you ever want to grab a meal or coffee, I'd love the opportunity to learn more about you and share more about our church. Hope to see you again this weekend!

After sending the message I just sit back and wait. The bait is in the water. In my experience half the time the response is overwhelmingly appreciative and they jump on the opportunity for lunch or coffee. A quarter of the time they respond graciously but do not seem interested in meeting. And then the final quarter are like ghosts. I don't really ever hear from them. It may be me, bad contact information, or they've already decided the church is not a fit for them.

The half who do engage are usually really sharp people. Not only are they engaging with me or our team and taking steps, but they are also experiencing the process they will be delivering to others as they begin to serve in the church showing value to others. Our extra efforts are modeling an intentional value for people that they, in turn, will live out and create the connection culture of the church.

Before we move on to the next chapter, an obvious question

might be "How do you get their information to do the fol-low-up?" I always start by thinking through this lens: Are they in our church database? Did they check a kid in, have a volunteer assignment, or fill out a Connection Card? If they did any of those, I have basic information. Now, as long as I make a note of their name, I should be able to find them in the system. Sometimes the opportunity presents itself to exchange contact information, and if they are open to it, that is the best way to know for sure. But this is delicate, and you really need to read the situation right, so we'll talk about that at length in this next section.

Understand Relational Pace

When you keep things cool, you show value to people by respecting their relational pace. Not space—be sure you catch that. *Pace.* Everyone is unique and their engagement temperature will reflect that.

Good connectors get better and better at gauging people's connection temperature. Some people are warm, and some are pretty cold. Some start cold and warm up gradually. Others need time to thaw, so you just let them sit a little.

Read people's body language and visual cues to gauge their temperature and see if they are open or closed for connection. The higher your EQ, or emotional intelligence, the better you will be at reading this. But there are some general observations anyone can grow to see.

Some people are obviously open. They match your eye contact, mirror your enthusiasm, and pause for dialogue. These people are warm and ready. Others are in between. They respond enthusiastically but stay in motion. They are open to connection but are in the flow of their focused objective (check kids in, get coffee, use restroom, find a seat). And finally, some are just closed, guarded, and a little prickly. They will be generally cordial to a greeting but show limited expression, limited eye contact, and no slowing down. Just let them keep moving, and maybe look to add value to them when they come to a stop.

Connectors keep things cool by learning to float a question rather than ask it directly. When you float a question, it's light, exploratory, and flexible—easy in, easy out. Then read their response. Based on their response you can ask a more definitive follow-up question. Connectors know how to explore, read, and follow up.

Direct: Do you want to go to lunch this week? (intense)

Exploratory: Maybe we could get together sometime? (relaxed)

Finally, add value by staying aware of what's going on in the environment and what their individual needs are. Be aware if they have kids needing to get checked in. Be aware if they are running late for service. Be aware if they are trying to meet up with someone who you can help them find. Sometimes it is better to add value by connecting them to their destination than connecting to you personally.

The emotional intelligence of a connector only needs to go up when connecting high-capacity leaders. We all need more leaders. In the next chapter, I will share with you how you can be intentional with leaders and connect more of them in your church.

Key Takeaways

- We must first ascribe value to the person before we can add value to the person.
- No matter how big your church is, when someone is greeted by name, it feels like home.
- Name memorization comes down to one thing: motivation.
- The three keys to remembering names are *listen, record,* and *reference.*
- Serving is the greatest way to add value to people.
- Make as many promises as you can keep.
- Our extra efforts are modeling an intentional value for people that they, in turn, will live out themselves and create the connection culture of the church.
- Understand relational pace. Good connectors get better and better at gauging people's connection temperature.

Reflection Questions

1. Would you consider yourself good at remembering people's names?
2. Do you have a good note-taking process to help you record names and key information to help you follow up with someone?
3. How could you get better at adding value to people you connect with by serving them and exceeding their expectations?

10

CONNECTORS ARE INTENTIONAL WITH LEADERS

He told them, "The harvest is plentiful,
but the workers are few. Ask the Lord of the
harvest, therefore, to send out workers into
his harvest field."

LUKE 10:2, NIV

We love harvest time. Big church weekends like Easter, Christmas, and Mother's Day are so exciting. There are new faces, full services, and powerful ministry moments. The church is just buzzing in all areas. But, as exciting as the harvest is, we also get stretched and are reminded of Jesus' instruction to *pray* because we need more workers.

Workers are the volunteer leaders who make a great church. Great churches are not built on the gifting of one singular leader or a super-gifted staff. They are built by the men and women who work jobs, raise families, and still make the time to "seek first His Kingdom and His righteousness" (Matthew 6:33a, NIV).

These workers are the leaders in the environment—leading Small Groups, children's teams, first impressions teams, ministry teams, and every other amazing volunteer team. They are the one's equipped by the staff, contributing to the vision, and taking care of the people. They really are the heartbeat of the church. Thank you if you are one of these leaders.

These leaders aren't easy to come by and they are definitely in high demand. When people ask my pastor where he gets such sharp leaders, he jokingly replies, "At the gettin' place." Obviously, there is no "gettin' place." You have to pray for them, select them, and train them. It's basic discipleship. There are no shortcuts.

—

Several years back, we hosted a men's night at our church called "Meat, Message, Mayhem." The whole goal was to put on an event that men would invite their unchurched friends to. Picture a sea of men spread across the parking lot playing tailgate games, competing in sport challenges, and scoring BBQ grill-offs.

Standing out amongst the crowd of men was a tall sharp dude sporting Ray Ban glasses, a pink polo shirt, khaki shorts, and Sperry Topsiders, just strolling about like a fish out of water. Most of the guys looked ready for a tailgate party and he looked ready for a Regatta.

No joke, my immediate thought, right or wrong, was, *If I don't connect with that brother, we'll probably never see him again.* I went up and introduced myself and told him to hang with me for the event. I found a couple of other guys like him, made sure connections were made, and thankfully he stuck around.

He ended up in my men's discipleship group and even co-led the next group with me. Now, several years later, he's a key leader in our church, a top supporter of the vision, a respected doctor in the community, and a good friend. He often reminds me of the huge difference that simple connection made on his life and his becoming the man of God and spiritual leader he was called to be.

I was able to make a personal connection with this gentleman, but that's not always the case. There are many times I meet someone and know that they need to be directed to another person. This may be a great lay leader or another high-capacity leader like themselves. Remember, a connector is not just connecting leaders to themselves but helping them find connections for life.

Leaders Stand Out

Often, leaders aren't looking for help, or necessarily presenting an open demeanor. They are trying to figure you out more than they are interested in you figuring them out. They may be a little more guarded than others and hesitant to open up. It's all good. In fact, it's great. These are often the leaders you need. It just takes a leader to lead a leader.

Leaders always take your environment to the next level. The leaders who intimidate you today are at another level than those who intimidated you a year ago. Continue engaging those who intimidate you and you'll keep lifting the leadership lid. As you grow in your personal ability to lead, your collective environment will grow in its ability to connect more leaders. More leaders allow us to love and serve more people.

Let's talk about what a potential leader looks like. They look sharp.

S.H.A.R.P. People

"We need more people like this!" If you've ever built a team or a culture, you've had this thought about someone you are excited about. For years I struggled through proper adjectives in describing a certain type of person who I was excited to meet on the weekend at church. I knew it when I saw it, and these people often became our best leaders. They would consistently prove to contribute the most to our environment and care for the most people.

What was it about these people that made them stand out? For whatever reason, I began adopting the word "sharp" to describe them to my team: "Did you meet Joe and Jan, the sharp couple, at the 9:30 service?" Many times, my team saw them too and would respond, "Yeah, I did. They were sharp!"

I found that it wasn't enough to just call them sharp. I needed to help my team see what I saw and really understand what I was looking for. I needed to answer the question "What is sharp?" What is the combination of external and internal indicators that are subconsciously producing this impression? So I broke down the word "sharp" to help explain what I see.

First, let me qualify that understanding people is such an art, and people are so unique. But here is a broad description I've found to be helpful to identify S.H.A.R.P. people. This breakdown is not exhaustive, of course, but I do think it is a great point of reference to describe these individuals:

SECURE - They are comfortable in their own skin and adapt well to their environment. They engage well with others and have a social awareness that puts you at ease.

HEALTHY - Physically, they have vibrancy; emotionally, they have stability. They aren't needy. They have life on them and light in their eyes.

ATTRACTIONAL - They draw people in. They attract others because of their personal security, confidence, and leadership.

RELATIONAL - They flow. There is a natural connection with them. They get along well with you, the same way they will get along with the next person they meet.

POSITIVE - The glass is half full, not half empty, and the future is bright. They can see the good regardless of the circumstances. They're full of faith.

I look at the SHARP leader description and my first thought is, *Man, I want to be more like that! I want to be SHARP!* This breakdown really helps us know what we can aspire to be and what we should look for in others. We must consistently grow ourselves to better serve others while inviting others to do the same.

Again, I want to clarify: I use the word "sharp" to describe the external expressions of strong internal qualities, not the external appearance of a person. We all know that someone can look like they have it together on the outside but be falling apart on the inside. We must look deeper to serve people at their deepest level.

Nobody has all of these SHARP qualities radiating all of the time. And even if someone does not demonstrate any of these qualities, we still make sure they are connected with and served equally. Remember, none of us is always as sharp as we'd like to be—we're growing.

If there was a precious commodity in the church, it's sharp people with a passion for Jesus and a heart for others. These men and women are the future Small Group leaders, rockstar children's volunteers, usher leads, etc. These are the leaders you need to ensure that everyone is served and loved well. They could be young or old, male or female, and every ethnicity on the planet. There's no stopping leadership; sharp just stands out.

When you first meet them, you may not know their character or their spiritual maturity, but what's obvious is their potential. They have qualities you can't teach and the foundation to build spiritual leadership. I'd much rather coach a natural leader into becoming a spiritual leader than build a leader from scratch. I'm willing to do both, but I also want to steward well those coming into our environment with a leadership gift. We need them.

You spiritually build the church with sharp leaders because they take care of people. They lead the teams, and they lead the leaders. Sharp people are the hardest to attract, but when you do attract them and connect them, they always connect other sharp people. Like attracts like, and like connects like.

Every weekend I'm connecting with everyone God places in my path, but my sights are unapologetically dialed in for sharp people. I want them to know Jesus and know our vision as soon as possible. The more workers, the greater the harvest.

Develop Your Connection Conscience

When talking about my focus on sharp people, I'm looking for leadership qualities that transcend superficial exteriors. Influence is more than affluence. I am also aware that leadership qualities are in great demand and those who have them often find themselves in positions of influence in the marketplace that lead to affluence.

If I am a leader connecting leaders, I must personally be responsible to not be preferential in my efforts to be intentional. Let me say that again: Being intentional is different from being preferential and that must be sorted according to your own conscience.

To further clarify, let me say this: I love generous, successful, life-giving people. They have big worlds and they invite you in. They always have extra seats for the game and theater tickets they're not going to use. They know people I want to know and vacation places I want to go. I think you see the picture I am trying to paint for you.

If I have the option of connecting with someone like this or with someone who zaps my energy and comes with more needs than gives, I know where my flesh is going to lean every time. And because of my local church influence, if I'm not careful, my world, or yours, could quickly be consumed with the former and box out the latter. We do not need to be friends with everyone, but we do need to serve everyone without favoritism.

Sorting through this pushed me to develop my own connection conscience. It's not a grid or evaluation method. It's a simple heart-check to help me have God's heart. The process of getting my heart right may be different from yours, but it's something a connector must keep in check. This is not a new thing for the church, but it is instruction James gave to the early church connectors:

> *My brothers and sisters, believers in our glorious*
> *Lord Jesus Christ must not show favoritism.*
> *Suppose a man comes into your meeting wearing*
> *a gold ring and fine clothes, and a poor man in*
> *filthy old clothes also comes in. If you show special*
> *attention to the man wearing fine clothes and*
> *say, "Here's a good seat for you," but say to the*
> *poor man, "You stand there" or "Sit on the floor*
> *by my feet," have you not discriminated among*

yourselves and become judges with evil thoughts?
JAMES 2:1-4, NIV

Until you establish your connection conscience, you will flounder through motives. You may overcorrect in one direction or another. In fact, people often find it easier to accept the person of modest presentation than the one with obvious means. Unfortunately, this is often done out of our own insecurity and exposes our desire to feel needed, liked, or superior.

When we choose to connect with someone we are comfortable with rather than with the person who intimidates us, we may even subconsciously be measuring ourselves against that person. And that is not wise according to Paul in 2 Corinthians 10:12.

The point is, we should not compare or show favoritism either way; but we should, with all equality and love, serve those God places before us. It is often fear, not favoritism, that causes us to show partiality in how we relate to people. If we are secure, we can be secure in our motives.

> It is often fear, not favoritism, that causes us to show partiality in how we relate to people.

When you trust your motives, others can too. If you honestly want more for people than from them, they will let you in. Someone may be rich in wealth and poor in health. If you can't see past their wealth, you can't pray for their health. Everyone has needs that money can't meet. Everyone is poor somewhere. Everyone is rich somewhere. What matters is how you treat everyone without showing partiality.

131

Connect People to the Vision

Always look for ways to connect people to the vision, not to yourself. The only long-term way to connect someone, especially a high-capacity leader, to the church is by connecting them to the vision—not another relationship, not a friendship with you, but the vision.

> The only long-term way to connect someone, especially a high-capacity leader, to the church is by connecting them to the vision.

The vision is the shared purpose that connects an individual to your church. It makes them part of the family, not just part of you. Too often I have made the mistake of joining someone to myself, not the vision of the church. And as soon as our relational proximity changed, they drifted from the church.

I've found you can only relationally prop people up for so long. I've tried to get better at making sure they are taking the steps to connect to the vision of the church, not simply myself or other relationships.

In the next section, I will share with you the process we have adopted and developed to connect people to the vision of the church.

Key Takeaways

- The harvest is plentiful but the workers are few. Pray for more workers.
- Leaders always take your environment to the next level.
- Look out for S.H.A.R.P. leaders: secure, healthy, attractional, relational, and positive.
- Leadership qualities transcend superficial exteriors.
- Do not show partiality but intentionality to ensure everyone is taken care of.
- The only long-term way to connect someone, especially a high-capacity leader, to the church is by connecting them to the vision.

Reflection Questions

1. Are you being intentional to pray for and connect leaders in your church? What are your top needs for a leader to solve?
2. What are your strengths as a S.H.A.R.P. leader and where could you most improve?
3. Are you confident in your ability to connect someone to the vision of the church and not simply to you relationally?

SECTION I

THE POWER OF CONNECTION

WHY connection is the
church-culture game changer

(For Everyone in the Church)

SECTION II

THE PRINCIPLES OF CONNECTION

WHAT you can do to be
a better connector

(For Volunteers & Leadership)

SECTION III

THE PROCESS OF CONNECTION

HOW to build a
connection process

(For Leadership)

THE PROCESS OF CONNECTION

**Think Like a Guest; See the Connection Card as Gold;
Follow a Follow-Up Process; Grow the Growth Track;
Track the Growth (the People Board)**

Process: noun, systematic series of actions directed to some end. (Dictionary.com)

I distinctly remember raising my hand in a meeting to ask a consultant, "So, what exactly is a process?" His time was expensive and he sure thought we needed one, but I didn't even know what one was.

Well, I do now, and I love them. In fact, here's why: A process is the best way of doing things that takes the highest level of thinking and experience and makes it scalable throughout the organization (and shareable with others).

In this next section, I will share with you processes I have learned from some of the best and have made better for us, and hopefully you can make it even better for your church. These are processes to move a first-time guest through a series of intentional steps to see them connected to Jesus, relationships, and the mission of your church, and to guarantee that no one falls through the cracks.

11

THINK LIKE A GUEST

*Let each of you look not
only to his own interests,
but also to the interests of others.*

PHILIPPIANS 2:4, ESV

Jesus lived His life completely focused on others. He is the ultimate model for us to follow. The apostle Paul encourages the church in Philippi to have the same mindset of Jesus by putting others first. One of the hardest things to do as a person, even as a Christian person, is to think of others and not just ourselves. But when we put others first, it's powerful.

A guest mindset is an *others* mindset. The key to serving guests who come to our churches is to see through their eyes. To be able to see through their eyes, we should ask ourselves, *What are they experiencing? What are they feeling? How can I meet them there?* When we put others first, we begin to love and serve people like Jesus. His heart comes out in our forethought and actions.

Everyone starts as a first-time guest. They'll have a first-time experience at your physical location, and even before so, on your website or online service. This is a unique moment of newness, anxieties, and unknowns. It doesn't matter if you are a seasoned Christian or a first-time church-goer, the first-time experience of anything can be daunting.

If you, as a leader in your environment, lose that sense of new-ness—if it becomes too common—then you will lose the empathy you need to connect well with guests. A great connection process starts with a great guest perspective. You have to do your best to think like a guest.

> A guest mindset is an others mindset.

Every opportunity you have in a new environment is an opportunity to get this perspective back. Recently, my wife and I checked into a hotel in Dallas for the first time. I was thinking, *Should I valet or self-park? Where do I check in? Where are the restrooms? Are they expecting me? Am I dressed like the other guests? Do I tip the guy unloading the bags or the other guy bringing them to the room?*

Granted, I am an environmentally anxious person. Anything new gets my heart rate up. I thrive in familiarity. I find peace in going to the same restaurant. I jokingly say I even plan my spontaneous moments. The idea of just going with the flow is an idea I seldom have. I get better every year, but I admit I am a bit of a control freak.

When you go somewhere new, you give up a degree of control, and that can be scary. Let me give you some thoughts to help you understand how comfortable you are with what you've become familiar with. Think about how you would feel if you were a first-time guest attending a worship service of a completely different religion. Imagine trying to fit in, follow the rules of the environment, figure out who is doing what, or understand what you are seeing. Think about how that would press on your anxieties.

Or when was the last time you drove up to a random preschool and handed your kids off to someone? Yikes! That's what guests may feel each weekend at our churches dropping kids off for the first time. It's their most cherished thing, and yet we have the expectation that it should be easy to trust us.

What is common to us is brand-new to our guests and we can't forget that. We haven't even talked about the guilt and shame that so many feel as they engage the church. It's a lot to overcome. However, we can orchestrate the best possible process to meet them where they are.

Recently, a sweet lady approached one of our greeters at the front doors and asked if she could come in. She was so grateful when she was warmly welcomed in. Think about that. We know our community is welcomed in—it's why we exist. But we can't assume they know this.

Everything Must Communicate to the Guest

Everything needs to be seen through the guest's eyes, not our own. Both to the first-time guest and to the regular attender, there should never be a thought of "it's obvious." That should be a thought we constantly challenge to make sure we are over-communicating.

Over-communicating is the beginning of communicating. There is no such thing as over-communicating. Being annoying? Yes. But over-communicating? No. There is saying, promoting, and posting, and then there is communicating. Communication isn't what you say; it's what is heard.

Before becoming a pastor, I worked in radio. I remember the program director constantly reminding the on-air personality that it takes saying something about ten-plus times before the listener hears it one time. When we get tired of saying it, they are just now hearing it.

My master's degree is in communication. I'm fascinated with the subject, yet I am constantly still having to remind myself to over-communicate. Just because you know something doesn't mean others do. Just because you said it doesn't mean they heard it, or at least heard what you meant by it. Just because there is signage doesn't mean they saw it.

Where should I park? Where do I enter? Where do I check kids in? Where is the restroom? Where's the Worship Center entrance? Where do I sit? How long is the service? Nothing is obvious; everything must be communicated by signage first and person second.

Signage is your friend. Good signage can make the experience for your guest so much easier and make it easier for you to serve them well. From the street to their seat there should be way-finding signage creating a trail of crumbs to follow.

If you distribute print pieces (bulletins, worship guides) or promote on the screens, remember that the person reading it is most likely new or newer. Let them know what to expect in regard to order and length of service. They know when it starts, but do they know when it ends? Make it clear in the announcements what their next steps should be. Every department will want to promote their activities, but weigh it heavily toward guest engagement opportunities, because that is primarily who is reading it.

> Communication isn't what you say; it's what is heard.

Don't only use insider language in service, in print, or on screen, but be clear to say what things are. So many of our names for things sound cool but aren't clear. Take the extra step to say the name of the event or environment and clarify what it is for the person hearing it for the first time. For example, rather than saying, "Come to Joy!" instead say, "Come to Joy, our Women's Christmas event." Likewise, don't say, "Your kids should come to Elevate," but, "Your kids should come to our student ministry service called Elevate."

Staying focused on the guest is the mindset we need to constantly stay in. Over-communicating is communicating. Until we are tired of saying it, they haven't even begun to hear it. Plus, importance is communicated by redundancy. The more you focus your messaging toward guests, the more your entire church will value their engagement. Yes, I am over-communicating this point.

Welcome and Greet Every Guest

There is a saying that goes, "You never get a second chance to make a first impression." That is so true and even more paramount in moments of anxiety and acceptance. Recruit and train to get your best people on the frontlines engaging those most impressionable in your environment. The greeters at the doors and the hosts online are the face of the church—the first face people see representing the personality of the environment.

In almost every membership club, it's the person at the door who waves you in or waves you off. The doorman/woman is the gatekeeper of the building. When people come to our church, we want to greet them with such genuine friendliness that they feel welcome before they have a chance to feel anxious.

When Gabrielle and I first visited Milestone Church in October 2002, a man named Michael smiled with the warmest smile and opened the door for us. When Michael saw us walking up, we knew he was excited to see us and wanted us to be there. This set the stage for our experience.

The greeter is on the frontlines of the first impression. They express the heart of the church. Before guests even come through the doors, they should know they matter to you and to God. Some of the ways greeters demonstrate this is through genuine engagement, service through opening doors, and a readiness to serve the individual.

Genuine engagement cannot be taught. I've tried training greeters and they do get better, but nothing is better than those who have the natural ability to just get it. If you are reading this, then you understand. I don't even need to explain. Identify individuals who have "it" and put them on your frontlines as greeters. Put the "people people" with the people.

We have a philosophy of service that a guest should never touch a door. We open it for them. I remember Zig Ziglar once saying he could count on one hand the number of times he saw his wife open a door, and she was one of the best door openers he knew. He was simply there to always open it for her. I remember how practical it sounded but how profound it communicated honor. I don't want our guests, or our members, to ever touch a door handle. It is a simple but thoughtful way to communicate value.

Finally, a greeter is often the first place for someone to ask a question. Usually, these questions require directional instruction and I don't believe we should ever point when we have an opportunity to connect. For this reason, greeters need redundancy at doors to make sure they can walk people to their answers.

A great customer-service philosophy is to walk with someone until sight is established, but I'd rather take them right to the spot. Sometimes you can even take them right to the person or resolution of their need. That really makes someone feel welcomed and valued. Even on online church platforms, hosts can take an extra step to get the link, the form, or the person right to someone rather than pointing them to an overwhelming website.

I learned a valuable lesson while working for several years in a high-end running store. Not everyone wants to have their hand held and not everyone wants help, but everyone wants to know help is available should they need it. It irritates me when someone is hounding me when I am looking around a store, but I'm equally irritated when I need help and can't find someone. There is an art to being available without being overbearing.

You have to get the "people people" in the right spots. I am reminded of my sister-in-law making a comment about visiting a church. She asked, "Is there a way I can guarantee that no one will talk to me?" What she was saying is that she needed a little space and didn't want an overbearing person making her feel bad about herself, her life, or her lack of churchiness. What she would be open to is a genuine, authentic, loving person who would accept her. She found that and is a part of a great church now with a heart to be that for others.

Establish Self-Identification Points

No matter what size your church is, the best way to serve a guest is to coordinate with the self-identification points. These are places where guests volunteer the fact that they are new. You're not guessing and they're not singled out. From these points, it's much easier to roll out the red carpet than it is to chase them around with it.

I want to go through a few of these that we have found to be incredible self-identification connect points. These are great places to add the most value by meeting some of the most obvious needs. There are a lot of places to connect and serve guests, but here are a few I want to highlight.

- Child Check-in
- Plan Your Visit Online
- Guest Parking
- Guest Tent/Room/Kiosk
- Early Seaters
- Front Receptionist

Child Check-in

Many times, I have seen churches focus on the function of child check-in and overlook the opportunity for connection. This can either be a great opportunity to add value or can create a point of frustration for a family. Think back to how you felt the last time you filled out forms in the doctor's office waiting room. Ugh! That's how they feel.

They may already feel out of place and then they are asked to recall birthdays and allergies all while their kid is rolling around on the ground. Not fun. It may be easier for you than for me, but I can't even handle a Chick-fil-A drive-thru with multiple orders being thrown at me by my kids.

For many parents, this also represents the first time they are leaving their kids in the hands of a stranger, the first time they face rejection in walking away from those watery eyes of abandonment. It's all good, a part of life, and an opportunity to love people well in a real milestone moment.

You also have the family that's worn out from the toll of finding a church home. Maybe it's the third week in a row the kids have been through this process, or it could be their first time ever going to church. This can be an emotionally and relationally (even physically) exhausting process.

Maybe they've been uprooted from the familiar and are still navigating the pain of transition. Who knows what they are coming out of. There is a lot going on, but again, it's our opportunity to love them well at the point of their need by getting them connected.

With all that said, you need a dedicated process for first-time-guest check-ins—a process that considers all of the above and makes it as easy as possible; a process that begins with clearly marked signage of where to go, and leaders ready and available to greet and confirm they are in the right place.

It is important to make sure your check-in process is doing its best to serve them and not you. I know there is valuable information you may never get if you don't ask now, but ask yourself, how important is it, really? Ask the minimum you need. Instead of asking how much good info we can get for our database, ask, what's the minimum we can ask and provide excellent child safety and emergency communication?

The child check-in forms need to be as efficient as possible, all while capturing the necessary info. Make sure that the person capturing it is fast at typing and that there is room on the form to fill it in with ease and the counter space to do so. Regular attenders should be kept entirely away from the guest process by having self-check-in stations that serve regulars best.

Guided Connection Tour

The guest should be walked to the kids' classrooms on a guided tour by a connector—someone who can quickly make them feel welcomed by making the kids feel special and the parents feel confident. They should identify the security zones, point out the restrooms and explain restroom protocol, cast the vision for the ministry, and brag on the great volunteers.

When they get to the classroom, they should introduce them to the teacher, relay anything learned about them in the short visit, and share any concerns of the parent or child. On the way back out of the kids' area, the volunteer should take the time to connect with the parents at a more adult level and help them with anything they should know about pick-up. Then the connector should guide them to their next place—show them where restrooms, coffee stations, classrooms, or worship centers are.

Welcome-Bag Identifier

We provide a Welcome Bag to every new family checking in at the children's check-in. This bag is full of comforts for them, like water, gum, mints, a pen, and information. The bag then also identifies them as first-time guests in our environment to make sure they get some extra love from our team and connectors. We don't want to be awkward or call them out, but we do want to be intentional to connect with them.

Over time, your leaders and members pick up on this and reinforce your culture of connection. We want to be kind and caring to everyone, how much more the person sitting beside you with the first-time-guest Welcome Bag? Noticing a Welcome Bag down the aisle has led to some of the greatest connections.

We also employ a special identification tool utilizing the check-in name tag for the first-time-guest kids. They get a special check-in tag that only our leaders are aware of, but it helps us serve our first-time-guest kids in a special way. We know how overwhelming it is to be new, so we go above and beyond to help them feel comfortable.

Plan Your Visit Online

A "Plan Your Visit" option on your church website is a great way for any guest to get a preview and overview of their potential experience—help them put themselves in the building. People will experience your church online before they make the decision to experience it live, so make it a great experience.

Give them all of the information they might need: service times, parking instructions, what to wear, service length, and order of events—prayer, songs, message, etc. Explain what is available for their kids. After you tell them, look for ways to show them.

Anything you can do to help them visualize will help them feel more comfortable, like links to videos of the service, the message, maybe even a fun video fly-through of the building—whatever you have that helps them see a safe, clean, fun, welcoming environment.

Finally, and this is a big one, provide a way for parents to fill out all the child check-in forms online and speed up the process. Use the simplest capture document possible with the minimum info, and then upload to your check-in software on the back end. This is a great way to serve guest families. Now your teams can be ready to welcome these families and even greet the kids by name.

We have even incorporated another feature where guests let us know exactly which service they are attending, what car they are driving, and even what drink they might like from our cafe. When we are at our best, one of our Guest Team members can meet them with their cafe drink of choice, greet their kids by name, and host them right into the building. That's pretty special. I'm so proud of our amazing Guest Team.

Guest Parking and Guest Team

What better way to communicate that you are excited for and expecting guests than having special parking for them? We have front parking, with easy access to the main entry, that intuitively says, "We thought of you. We hoped you would come! We saved you a spot. The best spot!" You should have such a great guest-parking experience that people delay membership just to keep the perk. Yes, I have heard that happen more than a few times.

The guest-parking self-identification point allows a Guest Team member an opportunity to provide a hosted experience right from the start. Even before they hit the doors and all of the unknowns, a host is there to answer questions before they are asked. You may help a young family to kids' check-in or an elderly couple to a sitting area, and along the way point out restrooms, coffee stations, and auditorium entrances.

Guest parking requires dedicated convenient parking spots. These can be permanent or temporary. You need good signage at every entrance to communicate where these spots are located. It has to be clear and obvious. We use red temporary signs, along with red banner flags, to help guests find their way.

As you grow, you may also want to use a combination of focused parking team members and specific signage: "New here? Turn on hazards/flash lights for Guest Parking." The key here is a parking attendant who is alert and ready to help direct them. That attendant makes the first impression on your campus, so you want it to be a welcoming one. (Note: If it's a quick turn from the main road to parking, then flashing lights is a quick method to alert a parking volunteer; whereas for a longer drive on property, it is better for signage to communicate using hazards to alert.)

Guest Tent, Kiosk, Room (Guest Suite)

I've seen tents, kiosks, and dedicated rooms all be great successes. Guest tents outside create a sense of buzz as you approach the building. They also help people get their building navigation questions answered even before they hit the doors. A well-marked Info Kiosk in the main commons area is great because it's an obvious place to find help and ask a question. The key here is to make sure the tent and kiosk are equipped with volunteers and information to provide answers to common guest questions.

A Guest Connection Room or Guest Central can also be a great place to serve guests. You have to experiment with it to get it to work for you. I've learned it works really well when the lead pastor is there after the service but not as well when they aren't. You should also communicate a motivating reason to go by, besides information and introductions, such as, "Come by the Guest Room after service and pick up a special gift we have for you."

Another concept we have loved introducing is the Guest Suite. The Guest Suite is a dedicated space we have at Milestone just off our commons/atrium where regular attenders bring their guests. From our guest data at Milestone, a majority of people come to church by way of invitation, so we created a place where members can host their guests well. We have this room stocked with drinks, candy, resources, books, Bibles, mugs, mints, gum, cookies, and coffee—all free for the taking.

In the room are also some of our best connectors and key staff.

We want it to be the place to be—the green room, the VIP room, the Admirals Club. We want our members to bring their friends to church and proudly bring them to the Guest Suite. Our pastor always wants to bless our guests, so we've just empowered our members with the resources to do the same.

Since it is a bit unique, let me describe our Guest Suite. It has nice finishes and furniture, wood flooring, rugs, art. It's not too big but it's warm, open to the flow of the commons, but closed off by glass for noise. The key is making sure it is a special place that draws and not an elite place that intimidates. We've found that there needs to be a good enough gift to give people a reason to get them there, but once they are there, they enjoy the simple hospitality items and helpful conversations.

Early Arrival Bulletin/Screen Readers

An overlooked guest identification point is in the Worship Center itself. Yes, it can be overwhelming once the service starts, but if you walk in five to ten minutes before service starts, it is a great time to connect. The regulars are still out visiting with friends; the guests are sitting alone in the seats.

To identify those new or newer, just look for those reading the bulletin or screens. You may call it a worship guide, bulletin, brochure, or service guide—if your church still passes one out, the people reading it are probably new or newer. (This is another good reason to make sure the content is guest-focused.) The same goes for the screens. I make a point to stroll the aisles before service and I often meet many new people.

Front Desk Receptionist

The church office is an incredible identification point. But too often, the receptionist is thinking about information and not connection. Make sure your receptionist is trained to not simply transfer calls to voicemails and forward emails but also to connect people with people.

I get so frustrated when I hear of someone contacting a church but not hearing back. That should never happen. We are called to *go* and make disciples, and these folks are actually *coming* to us wanting to "be made"! What an opportunity. A poor follow-up or no follow-up process must be solved.

Empower the receptionist with the tools for connection and not just deflection. They need to know where they go with the sticky questions that come their way. Where do they refer the person needing benevolence, selling printer services, and especially the person needing pastoral help or looking for hope? They don't need to solve it personally, but they do need to connect them to a person, or a clear process, that can.

—

When you think like a guest, you can meet them where they are and help them find their way in your church. More than getting people to places, it's personally connecting with faces and making them feel welcomed.

But for every guest we get to meet face to face, there are many more we missed sitting in the crowd. So how do we identify them? How do we serve them? That is what I will share with you in the next chapter, with the hope that we do not miss one guest who is looking to be connected in our churches.

Key Takeaways

- A guest mindset is an *others* mindset.
- A great connection process starts with a great guest perspective.
- Everything needs to be seen through the guest's eyes, not our own.
- Communication isn't what you say; it's what is heard.
- From the street to their seat there should be way-finding signage creating a trail of crumbs to follow.
- The more you focus your messaging toward guests, the more your entire church will value and be involved in their engagement.
- First-time-guest self-identification tools are helpful: guest parking, child check-in, "Plan Your Visit" online, welcome kiosks, welcome tent, Guest Suite.

Reflection Questions

1. When was the last time you entered your church thinking through the lens of a first-time guest?
2. Is your signage up to date in the building with language that is clear?
3. Do you have clearly marked and accessible self-identification opportunities for guests?

12

SEE THE CONNECTION CARD AS GOLD

Whoever can be trusted with very little can also be trusted with much, and whoever is dishonest with very little will also be dishonest with much.

LUKE 16:10, NIV

Every church needs an easily accessible communication tool that allows guests to provide their information and for regular attenders to keep taking spiritual steps. We call ours the "Connection Card." Every submitted Connection Card presents a stewardship test. How much do we care about the guest who has given us their information for the first time? How much do we care about the spiritual decision someone has acknowledged or the prayer request submitted by a member? God is trusting us with this person, this family. I believe God will send as many as we can serve, and that process, many times, starts with a Connection Card.

I was at a conference several years back when they passed out profiles of children needing sponsorship. After they cast the vision for sponsorship, they said, "If you are not going to sponsor the child whose picture and profile you are holding, make sure you return it to an usher. That profile is their one shot for sponsorship." I suddenly felt the weight of that card. In a similar way, I look at every single one of our Connection Cards as someone's one shot at being adopted into a spiritual family. It is so important to feel the weight of it.

The Connection Card is the currency of connection. It is the most important tool you have. From this card, we learn who's new, who's making a salvation decision, who needs prayer, and who wants to take a growth step. Use a card, use an app, use a text response, but this connection capture is essential. We have even included a QR code on the card itself to make the digital option easily accessible and have used a text-in number where the digital form comes right to their phone.

An important note to remember is that the Connection Card is not only about guests. As your church continues to grow, it is the easiest way for your entire church to engage in their next spiritual step or to find help with their need(s). If they can put it on the card, then help, prayer, and connection can come back to them.

You have to love the Connection Card. Treat them like sacred documents. Guard them, revere them, and fight for the potential of every one of them. Every single card is a treasure. Each one represents a person, a family, a soul. The cards are embedded with little clues to serve people and show them the love of Christ. We must be faithful with every one of them. (See a Connection Card sample in the appendix.)

More Cards = More Connection

Capturing people's information can happen in a variety of places. A welcome tent, info kiosk, or kids' check-in desk are great. An online service chat stream is good. But I am convinced the worship service is the best place to highlight and collect the Connection Card. Here you have the best opportunity to communicate to the right audience. This is where they will have the most time to fill something out without rushing. In the service is also where each and every person has a chance to use this card to inquire about their next step or to share needs. Remember, the Connection Card is not just for first-time guests but for everyone who wants to engage.

> The Connection Card is the currency of connection.

The guest welcome and Connection Card announcement is not only vital to serve guests, but it is also critical to the culture of the church. Through this announcement each week, we subconsciously focus the whole church to celebrate the one who is new.

A welcome announcement conveys that we expect guests. Without saying it directly, we communicate, "We aren't selfish. We aren't closed off. We are a growing family and we welcome you to be a part of it!"

I remember a pastor once telling me they don't do a guest welcome because they don't have many guests. Exactly! That's part of the problem. The guest welcome is not just an announcement but a culture reinforcer and vision we cast every week.

The growth or engagement results you are getting now have a direct correlation to the number of Connection Cards that are turned in. When the number of Connection Cards goes up, church growth and engagement increase. Take a minute to make sure you understand that before I continue. Do you believe you could double the growth and engagement by doubling the number of people you are following up with? I do.

I so believe this that I have tracked the weekend Connection Card metrics for years. Every weekend, along with attendance, we track the number of cards turned in and who was the service host/pastor on the mic. If someone is not good at getting Connection Cards turned in, they get coached to get better, or they don't get to host.

Our service hosts are authentic, genuine, and true to their own personalities, but they stick to a general script. For years I played with language and tracked results to find what produced the most Connection Card participation. You may be thinking, *You're crazy!* Maybe I am, but you can benefit from it. I've worked hard to figure out why even the most church-resistant, information-guarding person might fill out a card. I know that once they do, we can serve them so much better. The question is, how do we get them to know that?

We need to convey that the card serves them, not us. I was at a store recently when the cashier asked for my phone number at the check-out. I said, "No, thank you," but what she said next changed my perspective. "That's fine, but just so you know, we don't sell your information; we just use it to locate your purchase in case you lose your receipt." I gave her my number because she gave me a compelling reason, a "why." She convinced me it was a process to better serve me, not themselves.

Clear communication and the promise of a generous gift are the keys to satisfying the "why" to fill out the Connection Card. Everyone is asking, "Why do I need to share my information?" We need to answer it. People have done a lot of crazy things for a free T-shirt, and filling out a Connection Card is one of them. T-shirts, mugs, gift cards, etc., are all ways to say thank you for coming, but they also give people a reason to give their information.

> When the number of Connection Cards goes up, church growth and engagement increase.

Just as important as a gift, you want to clearly communicate what they can expect when they give you their info so you can lower their anxiety. It needs to be clear that you will not be showing up at their house at dinner time, selling their information, or spamming them with calls and emails. That's what has happened every other time they've given their information, and you need to give them a reason why they should trust you.

The Connection Card Announcement

What I am about to say is for a very small segment of the

population, but I would be so grateful to all for some collective empathy at least. Here it is: service hosting is hard. The service host is not the person preaching, not the person singing, but the person who brings connection in the room through all of the hard transitions in a service. They are the ones on the hook to smooth over mic malfunctions, technical delays, or power outages. They have to be ready for just about anything.

This same person, better than anyone else, needs to radiate a passion for first-time guests and for steps of engagement in the church. They need to know their role. It's not to be liked, not to be the lead pastor, but to help people take steps.

I have made the Connection Card announcement more than 1,000 times in the last 19 years. I've been asked several times by other staff team members, "How do you stay excited and authentic when you say relatively the same thing every week?" I tell them this: I don't figure out how to get excited about welcoming guests to every service; I *am* excited. The day I am not excited is the day I need to turn it over to someone else or get myself re-excited.

To make sure I keep excitement and authenticity as a service host, I make sure I personally meet a guest every service, every weekend, before I go on stage to greet them corporately. I do this without exception. This is a great advantage to a growing environment. Guests are coming in, and you always know there are guests in the audience. You can own your greeting with genuineness because you know you are talking to someone. Even if you don't see a guest to meet, at least meet someone new and it will freshen your delivery.

This Connection Card needs to be authentically acknowledged from the stage every weekend. It needs to be a priority in the service to show guests how they can engage, to show regulars the steps they can take, and to allow everyone to present prayer requests and needs. No matter how big a church gets, if it gets written on that Connection Card, someone needs to see it and follow up accordingly. It's a lifeline.

Every time you announce the Connection Card, you are "re-visioning" your church that we are about reaching people. We exist for those not yet here. We love the ninety-nine, but we are looking for the one, especially the one who came to our house. We prioritize this welcome every week in the service because it is important to God and to us.

I try to involve the whole church in the guest welcome each week. I say things like, "On behalf of the Milestone family, I want to let you know how honored we are to have you here today. In fact, if you were just to mention to someone sitting around you it's your first time, it would totally make their day." Now it's got the entire church engaged in the welcome, not just some host on a stage. That's really what we want: our awesome people welcoming other people, not just the stage host.

Here is almost exactly what I say with subtle variations from week to week:

> Good morning, Milestone! What an awesome time of worship. It is so good to be with you and with those of you joining us online as we continue [name of series]. On behalf of our Milestone family, I want to say a special welcome to those of you who are joining us today for the very first

time. It's always a highlight of our weekend when we get to meet someone like you here for the first time. (I met so-and-so from . . .) Maybe you're new to the area or just new to Milestone, whatever the case, we're so glad you're here with us.

I want you to know, we've put together some information we think you may find helpful coming into a new environment like this. We also have a fun gift for you—a little gift card, something we believe you will be excited to receive when you get it.

We'll send all this to you; all I need from you is some basic information. At some point during the service, please fill out the Connection Card sitting in the seat back in front of you. We'll keep your information protected; we won't show up at your house or bother you with a bunch of phone calls. We will simply send you a fun gift and some helpful information. Hopefully you'll take a next step with us when you are ready to do so.

We'll have a time of giving later in the service, and when the containers come by, just drop that card in there. Let that be your gift to us today.

Also, Milestone, if there is a step you are ready to take or a way we could pray for you, or any way we can help you, simply let us know. Our staff and prayer team will be praying for you this week!

The Connection Card Point Person

The Connection Cards come in through offering containers, giving boxes, kids' check-in, and the guest kiosk, but where do they go? Who gets the cards? What do they do with them? Do they think about each Connection Card like Jesus thinks about each sheep?

There needs to be one point person responsible for all of the Connection Cards—someone who treats them like gold and burns with connection, someone making sure that all of the collection points have in fact turned in their cards. This person can almost sense if a collection point has been neglected. They are dialed into the natural seasons of growth for your region. They know the difference between casual follow-up for an out-of-town cousin and a committed follow-up for a first-time guest from the community.

This may be the lead pastor, an associate pastor, staff member, or key volunteer. The size of the church will determine who has the capacity to give this the proper attention. When the church is young, or experiencing slower growth, the lead pastor may have the time and desire to look through every card. As the church grows, no matter the size, fight to ensure there is someone who wakes up thinking about the Connection Card.

Up to around 700 in attendance, our lead pastor was making phone calls to many of our first-time guests because he was the one most passionate about these people getting connected. Every staff meeting, he would list names on a whiteboard from those Connection Cards and determine who else would be best to follow up and serve these individuals and families. It was about that time he entrusted the passion and stewardship of this follow-up to me.

The Connection Card point person must burn white-hot for connection and keep the rest of the team hot on the importance of this information. They hold the line on data integrity and accurate information. They are pastoral in nature and empower administrative people around them. This person is the gatekeeper of growth. If they drop the ball, you are in serious trouble. But if they get a burden for it, it's explosive.

Treat first-time-kid's registration information the same as Connection Cards. I was reminded of the importance of this at lunch recently with a new couple that joined our church. The wife commented that she was perplexed they had received a kind welcome note and gift card upon their first visit but had never filled out a Connection Card. I simply commented, "But you checked your kids in." She said, "Oh my goodness, you guys are amazing!" I don't know about all that, but we can be intentional to serve people to the best of our ability.

—

I am going to tell you exactly what the point person needs to ensure gets done with the Connection Cards. They may not be the one doing it, but they must ensure it gets done to the best of your church's ability. This may be oversimplified, but the process is to *get eyes on the cards, enter accurate information in,* and *send helpful information out*. Let's take one at a time.

1. Get Eyes on the Cards

Never underestimate the power of putting your eyes on every card. You just feel the weight and responsibility of it differently.

It's like the difference between paying with cash or paying with a credit card. You just feel the cash in your hand differently. Many people push the data entry away from the follow-up/connections teams, but you want to keep it close.

I know it would be more efficient to have a data entry person collect it all, dump it in an excel document or in a church database, and just pull the report for our follow-up/connection teams, but I think we miss something. I know everything is moving digital and it streamlines nicely, but we do lose some personal touch when we lose the freehand.

Someone who is part of connection/follow-up needs to look at that card with their eyes, looking for what God might show them to help serve this person. You may see some extra notes in the margin, a prayer request, an address or neighborhood that stands out. You see if they are local or just visiting. You see their style of handwriting and get a small sense of their personality. I can't explain it—you just see it differently, and you serve them differently.

The goal of this exercise is to super-serve people. Surprise and delight. Look for ways to get outside of the routine follow-up communication process and do something personalized that communicates value. The more sincere and intentional you are, the more likely you are to create a warm connection.

2. Enter Accurate Information In

Once eyes have been on it, the Connection Card info has to be entered in. The software or program it is entered into may vary greatly by church and size. As early as possible, adopt a church management software that works for you.

The information going from the Connection Card into the computer has to be done right. From that point forward, whatever is in the computer is what lives on. If the email is entered wrong, they won't get the information. If the phone number is wrong, we can't follow up. If the address is wrong, we get "return to sender." Then the biggest problem is that we aren't able to keep our word that we said we'd be following up.

I still have feelings of angst thinking back ten years ago when we didn't communicate well to a few months' worth of guests because we didn't enter their "first visit date" correctly when entering the Connection Card info. You only make that mistake once, hopefully, but make sure it's not once per new staff member or volunteer.

This team may be trained volunteers, but they must feel the weight and be trained well along with staff doing this. Just put someone on it who really cares about how it's done and not just about getting it done.

3. Send Helpful Information Out

They trusted us with their information; now we can send them the best possible information to serve them—something that says, we see you engaged with us, we value you, and we want you to come back. This is not customary; this is a huge opportunity to meet them in their world.

Even the most basic communication is far more than a form letter or email template. It's their first personal communication from the church. That is a big deal. We should labor over this communication to make sure it is conveying the heart of the church and leadership.

This communication needs to be as warm and personal as possible while giving simple next steps. We also follow up with a "wow" in the mail to show we really do value them. This is unique to every church, region, and demographic, but I will share with you what we have sent out as important communication and memorable gifts to our guests.

Because it is so important, I will take the next chapter to lay it out fully and share some of the tools we use.

Key Takeaways

- The Connection Card is the currency of connection.
- The Connection Card is not only for first-time guests but for everyone in the church who wants to engage.
- The stage guest welcome is not just an announcement but a culture reinforcer and vision we cast every week.
- When the number of Connection Cards goes up, church growth and engagement increase.
- Clear communication of what to expect and the promise of a generous gift are the keys to satisfying the why to fill out the Connection Card.
- There needs to be a Connection Card point person who thinks about each Connection Card like Jesus thinks about each sheep.

Reflection Questions

1. Are you happy with your current Connection Card or similar guest information card tool?
2. Does your announcement make a good case for why a guest should be willing to complete a Connection Card and trust you with their personal information?
3. Is there a dedicated point person who goes through every physical card and is the steward over the follow-up process?

13

FOLLOW A FOLLOW-UP PROCESS

*Dear children, let us not love with words or
speech but with actions and in truth.*

1 JOHN 3:18, NIV

It's not enough just to say we care; we need to show we care.
A follow-up process is a follow-through on the promise we
made to serve our first-time guest. We want to do all we can to
express the love of God and love of the church toward these new
people visiting. It may be their first time at your church or *any*
church, so this is a special opportunity.

My starting thought with a follow-up process is the idea of
throwing a lifeline to every guest who visits our church building or visits an online service. Some are out there just floating
along, some are swimming, but there are some who are really
drowning. If we throw the rope, anyone can grab it at their point
of need. We just need to make sure we get the rope in front of
all of them.

I remember the first time I started learning about church follow-up and the whole assimilation process in the mid 2000s.

This process explained how to move someone from the crowd to the core. I loved the idea that we can create a process that takes care of every person and clearly communicates next steps to them. (Side note: That's when I had the first thought of being an "Assimilation Pastor." That title sounded dangerous in its full and abbreviated form, so thankfully we came up with "Connections Pastor" instead!)

Even more than what we communicate through the follow-up process, the intentional process itself communicates our value for people's growth and engagement. The responsive timing, intentionality, clarity, and whatever "surprises" we include say just as much as what we are actually saying. We don't just say we care and value them; our process can make them feel it.

—

Let's start by talking about a process to effectively follow up with all of the special first-time guests who completed a Connection Card or provided their information at Kids Check-in. They may have even been attending for a few weeks, but this is the first time they fill out something to let us know. This is a big deal.

Step 1: A Timely Thank-You

The sooner you can acknowledge and thank a guest for visiting, the better. Our team has a goal of sending this communication out by midday Monday, but you may do better. The timing itself communicates a lot before we've said anything with words.

It says, "We see you. We recognize you've taken a step to be known. We're glad you came. We received your information. We are organized. We are excellent. We have a process in place to take care of you."

For years, this initial communication was a mailed letter—now it's an email. (We still mail something to their house; I'll tell you about that next.) You can mail, email, or text—this initial communication is really up to you and what you think is best. For a season, we did a combination of both because not everyone gave us their email. Most everyone provides an email now, and it allows us to communicate efficiently while also providing helpful links. Text is even quicker now, but for many this is still sacred space. We will be moving to texting a short thank-you video very soon.

I anticipate that in the near future, we will have more intuitive apps and online tools for guests to opt in to and be noticed immediately rather than wait on correspondence. (Think about how Amazon knows you.) The best way we will serve them is by tailoring the information to get them what they want, and would want, if they knew about it. If a mother of grade-school kids is entering the information, she will not only receive back general church info but also children's resources and an invitation to the upcoming women's event. She could get directly connected to another woman in the church who's the same age, with children of the same age, to answer any questions she might have. The possibilities are endless.

But let's get back to our current reality and best practices. Besides a timely acknowledgment, the key to the initial communication is to thank them for coming, give them a reason to come back, and invite them to a place they can be known. I will break down the why behind each one of these.

First, *thank them for coming.* This is so important because they don't know how we feel about them yet. We need to tell them we are glad they came and that we would love for them to keep coming. They don't know what we think of them or their visit until we tell them.

Second, we want to *give them a reason to come back.* You can do this by promoting the message series or an upcoming special event or something special for their kids. You have to give them a compelling "because" to their "Why should I go back?" question. "Come back this weekend *because* we are . . ."

Third, this is a soft invite in this initial communication, but point them to the first class in your Growth Track, *the place they go to be known* and get to know more about the church. It's so important to have this class/gathering to point new people to. We'll talk about this in the following chapter.

This email/letter/text is best coming from the lead pastor because they may have already heard them share the weekend message and, ultimately, they will be the one they are most familiar with. Others may be more involved in the follow-up process, but because your lead pastor represents the leadership of the church, their signature is what you want at this point of communication. If you are sending a text, because it is a more personal space, it may be best to send it with a generic signature, such as "The _____ Church Team."

Communication needs to be to-the-point but as relational as possible, while reflecting the voice of the lead pastor and the culture of the church. If your pastor and church culture are super casual, then your communication should be really conversational with probably too many exclamation points and too many uses of "excited." You may be chill, relaxed, scholastic, old-school, whatever—just make sure it sounds like you and is reaching your intended audience.

Sample guest follow-up email:

FROM: MILESTONE CHURCH
SUBJECT: THANK YOU!
TO: [FIRST-TIME GUEST EMAIL]

Dear [First Name],

Thank you for being our guest at Milestone Church! We are honored you made the time to come be with us. I hope you were warmly greeted and enjoyed the service. Here's a link [include link] to the message if you want to watch it again or share it with a friend.

We hope you'll come back and join us again this weekend as we continue our series, [Series Name]. We all face issues in life that challenge us, whether it's a transition, loneliness, work, or feeling overwhelmed. But did you know that God wants you to live well in every season of your life, through the good and the bad? This series will help equip you to live well through the most common challenges we all face.

I want to also personally invite you to join me for our Discovery 101 class happening Sunday, [Date] at [time]. Discovery 101

---

is designed to help you learn more about the story and vision of Milestone Church. Lunch and childcare are provided. You can register online [live link] or just show up. I would love the opportunity to meet you and hear your story!

We look forward to seeing you this weekend,
[Lead Pastor Signature]

Step 2: A Surprise in the Mail

Who doesn't like a surprise in the mail? With everything going digital, there is something even more special about getting a hand-addressed envelope in your mailbox. You know it's either a thank-you card, a wedding invitation, or a birthday card. What you probably weren't expecting was a fun gift from a church. Surprise!

I think it's so important to do things like this to get out of the pile. Creating a "Wow!" takes more time and more money, but it also communicates more value. It tells someone, "You matter. You matter to God and to us."

In the history of our church, we've sent all sorts of things to create a surprise: Starbucks cards, Sonic cards, now we are sending Chick-fil-A gift cards that are full meals for the whole family. My rule for the gift is that it really has to be a "give"—no coupons, no marketing tricks to get you to come in and spend more money, but a real gift from the church that is good stewardship but also generous. Finding that balance is largely dependent on the context of your church.

The communication in the handwritten note needs to be focused and concise to keep the recipient's attention. It also helps to keep it short for the efficiency of the person writing it. Answer why we are sending a gift to them, and point them again to the first step in your Growth Track. (We'll talk more about the Growth Track in the next chapter.) The author/signature of this handwritten note is really up to you. Even though it is representing the heart of your lead pastor, as the size of the church grows, the believability of them writing it is lost. It can come instead from the connection team, pastor, or leader who will help them take steps, or simply the "Church Name" Family.

Handwritten Note Sample:

Hello!

Here is a little something to say thank you for being our guest! Also we'd love to meet you at our next Discovery 101. This class will help you connect with others and learn more about Milestone Church. Hope to see you this weekend, and please come say hello!

[Connections Pastor/Associate Signature]

Step 3: Personalized Follow-Up

A form email with helpful links is great, and a handwritten note with a fun gift wows, but there is even another level—a personal follow-up. I am talking about someone reaching out regarding a specific need and making themselves personally available to serve that need. This is over-the-top, second-mile service that makes connection so powerful.

You have to think differently about the information that comes in from a Connection Card. It's not "How do we make the process work as efficiently for everybody?" but "How can we personalize the follow-up for as many as possible?" With a little intentionality, the basic information can lead to a remarkable impact. Here are some ways you can personally follow up on prayer requests, comments, and next steps.

Prayer Requests

> Don't just pray for the prayer requests that come in; look to be the answer.

Don't just pray for the prayer requests that come in; look to be the answer. If someone is lonely, help them find a friend or Small Group. If they are looking for a job, think about who you might connect them to. If someone is in a financial struggle, get them in a stewardship class or with a budget coach. If they need prayer for their marriage, get them a marriage mentor. Yes, pray for them but also help them.

Comments

People often make comments on the Connection Card that give

us clues to help connect them. If someone mentions they are new to the area, follow up to see how you can help them find a house, school, dentist, grocery store, shop, etc. We can even help them get their kids registered for camps to help them make friends. We can do so many things to personally help them specific to their situation.

There may even be a complaint we can follow up with. I love what guest experience expert Danny Franks says in his book *People Are the Mission*: "Criticism is a gift we receive from our guests. Whether it's criticism of our programming, our processes, our people, a critic is like a free consultant who can help you see blind spots and make improvements."[15] These comments serve us and in turn we can serve others better.

Next Steps

When people check a box for a Growth Track/Next Step class, they are only halfway there. A formal email with confirmation details gets them to about 65 percent. However, when you follow up personally and let them know that you are excited for them and expecting them, it shoots up closer to 80 percent. Our extra effort communicates the value of these steps and how much we value the person taking them.

—

Those were a few examples but the big picture is this: extra effort leads to extra connection. There is a direct correlation between the energy you invest in someone and the connection they experience in church. We can't do everything for everybody, but when we do all we can, people feel loved and served in a special way.

The best place to focus your energy and attention is helping as many as possible get into the Growth Track. These are intentional classes that make growth and engagement accessible to everyone. In this next chapter I will share how a Growth Track is not only a great discipleship tool in your church but also a gift

Key Takeaways

- Even more than what we communicate through the follow-up process, the intentional process itself communicates our value for people's growth and engagement.
- Besides a timely acknowledgment, the key to the initial communication is to thank them for coming, give them a reason to come back, and invite them to a place they can be known.
- Creating a "Wow!" takes more time and more money, but it also communicates more value.
- Don't just pray for the prayer requests that come in; look to be the answer.
- There is a direct correlation between the energy you invest in someone and the connection they experience in church.

Reflection Questions

1. Evaluate your current follow-up process. Is it hitting the mark, or could there be some improvement?
2. What would be a great "Wow!" follow-up gift to send first-time guests?
3. How could more personal attention and more dedicated resources improve the follow-up process?

14

GROW THE GROWTH TRACK

But grow in the grace and knowledge of our
Lord and Savior Jesus Christ. To him be glory
both now and forever! Amen.

2 PETER 3:18, NIV

It's one thing for a church to grow in attendance, but something altogether different for it to grow in its values, mission, and culture—to grow the people. From the early days of Milestone Church, Pastor Jeff would say, "I don't want Milestone to grow into a church that I don't want to go to." He didn't say that out of self-interest but out of a desire to grow a little slower—to grow people a little more intentionally, and more united behind the values and mission.

When one's passion is to grow people and not just attendance, the church grows into a greater expression of its values and also grows in attendance. Maybe not as fast as we'd want because there are so many people we want to reach for Jesus, but it's a proven strategy that even Jesus modeled. Twelve disciples didn't look too impressive at the time, but it was the long play, a winning play.

That said, there needs to be a clear pathway to grow people so they can then help the newest people engage and grow as well. The heart of this is discipleship, not a program. It's simply a process to help make disciples who make disciples. This is the value of a Growth Track.

A Growth Track is a series of classes with intentional teaching and connection to facilitate spiritual growth and engagement. Along the way, we help them discover their unique spiritual gifts and provide opportunities for them to use their gifts for God by serving the church and community. As they complete their steps in the Growth Track, they can now begin to help others take their steps.

There are several amazing models of these intentional growth steps. I remember the simplicity of the "Four Bases" Pastor Rick Warren laid out in *The Purpose Driven Church* I read back in the late '90s. Pastor Chris Hodges and the Church of the Highlands team have brilliantly simplified a Growth Track with four spiritual steps adopted by hundreds of churches. At my own church, from week one until now, Pastor Jeff has championed a simple and clear process for people to engage, grow, and get connected.

The Growth Track being championed by the lead pastor is a key point that must be called out. From the top of the organization and throughout, everyone needs to believe the Growth Track is the lifeblood of the church, not simply a side ministry in the church. It super-serves those newest to the church by providing them an on-ramp of engagement that feeds all of the other ministries.

As people engage in our Growth Track, I often hear them say to our team, "Thank you for your intentionality." That's what a Growth Track does—it says we have a plan for your growth and connection. Every guest is unique, but in general, most people are looking to learn about the church, take some spiritual steps, and make some friends.

I will be very practical and to-the-point in this section. I will explain how we get people into the Growth Track through relational connection and intentional communication. I will explain how we move them through the process and launch them into Small Groups. I will not be going into great detail on how we expect God to move in people through the Growth Track, but please understand that spiritual growth is the goal. Finally, I will focus my attention on a Growth Track process for a physical campus, not an online campus. However, I do think there are many things that will carry over online.

Think Funnel

The key to any Growth Track is the funnel principle—everything moves from wide to narrow. You want to start as wide as possible (wide in frequency, content, accessibility, commitment). The wider you start, the more people you can get in and the more will come out. People are going to drop out with successive steps—attrition will happen—so make it as easy as possible for as many as possible to get in the top of the funnel.

This book is an example of what I am talking about. If you made it to this section of the book, you are at the bottom of the funnel. We started really broadly about the "why" *power* of connections, moved into some of the "what" *principles,* but here we are in the "how" *process* of connection. Only those who are serious about implementation and leading in this area will make it to this section. If I had started here, *you* would have liked it a lot better probably, but the majority would have checked out. (We can talk about them; they're not here anymore.)

The same funnel applies to your Growth Track. Start with the basics of what you want everyone to know and then move toward more specifics. This could be progressive steps for discipleship, commitment, involvement, and leadership. The Growth Track is like an amazing discipleship factory that makes super Small Group leaders, rockstar volunteers, dedicated disciple-makers, and awesome people who carry the values of your church.

Think Focus

Everything starts with the Growth Track. It is everyone's first step. Once someone is attending on the weekend, their next step is not a Small Group, serving, or another ministry environment; it's the Growth Track. Everyone starts with the Growth Track, and everyone communicates that to everyone who hasn't started the Growth Track.

It sounds simple, but communication alignment pointing everyone to the Growth Track is an all-out fight. It's an ongoing effort to champion the Growth Track to keep it the focus. You may even be fighting me right now as I try to focus you.

There are three key areas to focus communication in the start of your Growth Track funnel: *stage communication, print/digital communication*, and *creating a culture of communication*.

Stage Communication

There is no better promotion in your church than the stage announcement. I am not talking about a menu of announcements that most will tune out but a clear authentic appeal to come be a part of the church. It's not "we think this will help you understand us better." Instead think, *What do they want?* Less of us, more of them. Here's a way I might communicate it:

> Coming into a new church you may have questions and are wondering how to get connected relationally. After learning from others new to the environment, we've devised a Growth Track to help answer some questions you may have, and we'll help you meet some other great people looking for some of the same things you are. The first step is Discovery 101, and it's coming up next weekend.

The key here, like the Connection Card announcement, is to keep it fresh and authentic. This is something that will come up often because the class may be monthly, so you'll be referencing it often. As long as step one is communicated well, there is no need to push the other steps from the stage very often. Remember, it's a funnel, but all of the focus of communication should be on getting them into the funnel.

Once they get to the first class/step/event in your Growth Track, you can begin to cast vision for the next step. And then the next step promotes the next step. That is why it is important to focus all of your promotion on the start. The more who start, the more who will finish.

Print/Digital Communication

The first announcement in the bulletin/service guide or screens every week should be pointing to the start of the Growth Track. Whatever that first class is called, it should have top real estate in your print and digital announcement mediums. The majority of the people reading the bulletin, watching the screens, and visiting your website are newer and need that step more than anything else.

Keep the copy short and compelling. Share what it is, when it is, and how to sign up. Information like length of class, childcare availability, and if a meal is provided will help individuals in their decision-making process.

As already stated in chapter 13, "Follow a Follow-Up Process," the guest mailing communication should always be pointing to the start of the Growth Track. Thank them for coming, invite them back, and invite them to start the Growth Track.

Culture of Communication

Ultimately, you will know your Growth Track communication focus is working when you begin to hear other people referencing it. When someone believes in something, they share it. The ultimate marketing question is, would you refer it to a friend? Church members should be excited to refer people to the Growth Track. If not, we need to work on some things and make it better.

I remember a season when I had to get one of our steps in the Growth Track out of the ditch. It had no momentum. People weren't exactly sure what it was, or how to explain it to others, and they were definitely not motivated to refer it to others. We had some leaders serving, but it was more out of duty than passion and it was losing momentum.

I realized our members didn't know how to cast vision for it because they didn't know the vision for it (even after they had completed it themselves). The question they and others were asking internally was, "Why should we/someone attend this class?" People seldom asked why out loud, but we still needed to answer with a compelling "Because . . ."

We needed to cast a concise, compelling vision, deliver on it with a great experience and great volunteers, and then trust participants to echo the vision to their friends. It worked, and I'll share more about that later in the chapter.

When friends, volunteers, and members communicate the Growth Track, it has far more weight than a stage or print announcement. When your culture believes in your Growth Track process, they will be the ultimate champions of it.

Think Aquarium

After thinking *funnel*, and *focus*, think *aquarium*. The larger your church gets, the harder it is to know where people are in the wide ocean of people—not just knowing they were at church, but knowing where they are personally, spiritually, relationally. Are they getting discipled? Are they even coming back week to week? Who knows? But if they were in a great aquarium, it would be so much easier to observe their progress.

When I think of the Growth Track, I think of it as a magnificent aquarium our team is able to look into and observe to best serve people. This becomes an amazing environment where we can create the best possible experience for someone. Here we can introduce them to people we know who they should know, place them in Small Groups specific to their season in life, help with specific needs, and see how they are developing spiritually.

For a short but impressionable season, we can really keep track of where everyone is. We know if they are coming back. They have immediate access to leaders and the relationship with those leaders. Their names are becoming known and their gifts are being recognized by others.

Along the way they are grouped together with other people who are in a similar life stage. They build relationships and spiritual foundations, and before long they are launched back out to the ocean; but it's a totally different experience because they are connected. Now several people know them, where they are, how they are doing, and can help them continue to take steps of spiritual growth.

Growth Track Steps

I will share with you an overview of the Growth Track steps we are using at Milestone but I want to qualify a couple of things first. For starters, our Growth Track at Milestone is an amalgamation of other churches' Growth Track processes, which were amalgamations of someone else's. It's not better than another but it is the best for our needs. We've adapted it to meet our objectives to connect people relationally and develop them spiritually in the context of our church culture.

I think this is the best way to approach it as you build or adopt someone's Growth Track model. Don't just change it to change it but to make it better for your context. To help you understand what we have done at Milestone, I will walk you through an overview of the three classes in our Growth Track: Discovery 101, Serve Team 201, and Values 301.

Discovery 101

- First Sunday of the month
- Following 11 a.m. service
- Taught by lead pastor/video/campus pastor
- One hour and thirty minutes long
- Childcare provided
- Box lunch/water on table
- Round tables of eight
- Host/connector at each table
- Pictures taken as they arrive

Our first step in the Growth Track is a class we call Discovery 101. This class is a great opportunity for new people coming in to learn what we believe and for us to learn more about them. I tell people we've done our best to take the key questions we usually get asked by people who come into Milestone Church and answer them all in one class.

The class is not just informational; it's spiritual. It's people becoming a part of the Body. Recently I learned the story of a lady named Angela who woke up one Sunday morning and decided to attend our Discovery 101 class. She felt the Lord was asking her to do it. She went on to share that she loved the class so much that she didn't want it to end. She got emotional about belonging to a church family and knew that it was so much bigger than just learning some information; it was about becoming part of a family. I love that.

Overview

We open the class by simply telling *Our Story*. We want them to know where we came from so that together we can continue toward where we are going. Our story is simple. People get saved and discipled and then reach their friends and family who get saved and discipled. We make a big point of that. The goal is that it continues on with them to see their friends and family get saved and discipled.

After sharing our story, the first teaching is a clear presentation of *The Gospel* and it blows my mind the responses we see. In every class, we see 10 to 20 percent of the class raise their hand in response to a prayer for salvation. It is an amazing sight to see and the ultimate highlight for those serving in the environment. Every time, we are humbled by God's saving power and grateful to be in a growing region and a church that's inviting.

After presenting the gospel and celebrating those who responded in faith, it's very natural now to move into what *Our Mission* is. We draw a super clear picture of the target, the bullseye, the win. We make it clear what we celebrate, what we stay centered on, and that is this: *make a disciple*. We invite them into the mission Jesus called us into in Matthew 28:18-20, the Great Commission. Our mission statement echoes that: "Reaching people. Building lives." We eliminate a lot of division when we keep everyone centered on the mission. Our mission is aligning with Jesus' mission.

The middle of the class is focused on *Our Beliefs* and statements. People need to know what you believe so that they can decide if they are in alignment. It is our beliefs that bond us together in the faith and it is important there is unity in the essentials. There may be some things that are categorically non-essentials but are strong convictions for your church that you may want to address in this section.

Next, we spend some time communicating *Our Values* and how we live them out. These are our core values, things that we hold dear and want those joining us to begin embodying. They are not aspirational values but real convictions we live by. For us, the Bible, Mission, Spiritual Family, Development, and Generosity are values we expect those joining our church to grow in valuing as well. We'll unpack these in the third step in the Growth Track: Values 301.

Finally, we do something that may seem unnecessary, but we spend some time on *Our Structure,* specifically church government. This is our leadership structure, staff, elders, and board of directors. We clearly lay out oversight and accountability. This is something we highlight because we do it and have been intentional to invite it in. This section is always a great value to higher-capacity leaders and leaders who may have come from challenging structures.

Finally, we invite them to join *Our Family.* We would love everyone to join our family, but we need to be clear that they've first joined Jesus (in the Body) and that they affirm our beliefs and statements (in unity). We walk them through some simple forms to ask about salvation, ask about water baptism (they do not have to be baptized to join, but we keep encouraging it as they take steps), and point them to sign up for their next step: Serve Team 201.

Flow

There is the class material of course, but a big part of the success of the class is the flow. We have many pastors and church leaders ask to come and see our Discovery 101 in action to get a sense of the flow. There are some intangibles, but I want to try as best I can to help you see it and feel it.

Following our largest service, guests arrive at the clearly marked location. Sharp volunteers begin to guide their experience from that point until they walk out the door ninety minutes later. We have a pre-registered line with pre-printed name tags and another line for walk-up registration. We ask them to put on their name tag and move toward the classroom, where we quickly take their picture as they progress in. There is not a lot of set-up, but we have a nice muted background and adequate front lighting to capture a good picture on an iPad.

Picture taking is one of the greatest decisions we've ever made. This picture (with name tag in frame) will be added to their profile in our church management software. Picture taking is the ultimate game changer because you now have the face and name of every person you are helping take steps, find groups, and start to serve. Trust me, only a couple mysterious people a year will deny the photo opp. (In the next section I will share with you how these pictures become our People Board, the single greatest connection tool we have ever implemented.)

After their picture is taken, our seating host walks them right to a table where a table host is ready to welcome them. Like a hostess at a restaurant, our team is making intuitive decisions to help seat people at tables where they will connect well. We seat from front to back, and do our best to seat them where they will be most comfortable. This means we may cluster by life stage, backgrounds, and commonalities to give them a head start on connecting.

Table Host

A key role in this class is the volunteers who are serving as table hosts. We sit at rounds of eight and include a table host at each of the tables. These are members, not staff, who are giving of their time to serve those newest in the environment by answering questions and getting them connected. They themselves have recently been through the Growth Track and can encourage attendees to keep taking steps.

The key skill set for these table hosts is emotional intelligence. They will need to be able to flow with a variety of personalities in a limited window of time. They need to be able to read people well enough to relate and help them feel comfortable. The table host needs to be relaxed, friendly, and gracious because these people are coming from all over.

A key role for the table host is to help people with the paperwork. Nobody likes paperwork, but the host can soften it and encourage participation. This is valuable information that you'll never get again and will help you really serve the individual.

At each table setting are preset class booklets, forms, and pens to make it convenient. We've learned to separate an *information form* from the actual *membership form*. We do this so we can still collect helpful information regardless of whether they commit to becoming a member at the close of class. This form separation was a great move by our team, and I strongly encourage it. It helps you better serve people as they consider membership.

As we close the class, we call out the forms from the stage, and the table host makes sure everyone has what they need. We encourage everyone, regardless of whether they choose to become a member, to complete the *information form*. Second, we encourage people to sign up for next steps in the Growth Track, Serve Team 201 or Values 301. Finally, we let them know that we would love for all of them to complete the *membership form* and become part of the family.

Intentional Follow-Up Meetings

The week following Discovery 101 we have a follow-up meeting, one of the most special and vital connection meetings we have. This is my favorite meeting. Our connections super-team of key staff and volunteers look at every name, every picture, every form, and we prayerfully determine next steps of connection for each individual.

Here are some of the things—the intel—we are looking for. First, we find out how they came and where they came from. We talk about their age, where they live, family dynamics, and what they do for a living. We then look at their spiritual history to see if they have committed their life to Christ or been water baptized. Many times, this section is blank or incomplete, and that gives us an opportunity for follow-up.

The big win for this meeting specifically is to be Spirit-led in selecting individuals to connect one on one with. Someone on our connect team will take them to coffee, lunch, or breakfast to hear their story and personally help them take a step. Not everyone needs this direct of a follow-up, only those who we have a good sense would be receptive to it. (Many people who get a call from the church think they are in trouble, so remember that when you reach out.)

Approximately 30 percent of the class is personally connected with by one of our staff or volunteer follow-up team members. We do it draft style and the person who makes the request, or has the most obvious natural connection, is assigned the follow-up. The information we have will help guide the connection. We want to make sure they are saved, baptized, taking next steps, and we then serve them or their family in a personalized way.

These one-on-one follow-ups are a key to us staying engaged with potential leaders who God brings into our environment. Many of these are the sharp dynamic transfers mentioned earlier in the book. It is great to identify them at the top of the funnel because they may need more vision casting to keep them moving through the Growth Track. They are generally busy and not looking for any extras in their life.

It sounds like I am in the weeds, but these one-on-one connections establish the relationships that cast the vision for greater engagement and activation of their leadership gift in the church. From these connections we cast vision not only for our Growth Track but also for our Men's and Women's Development Groups. These are intentional groupings of hand-selected leaders, led by someone who has already been through a Development Group. The leader takes them through an incredible multi-week development resource, *The Way to Win*, by Jeff Little. These groups are one of the greatest things we do at Milestone to raise up leaders who follow Jesus, serve, give, and carry the vision. (See the appendix for details on Development Groups.)

Finally, regarding the Discovery 101 follow-up meeting, we want to help everyone with a specific step that moves them into relationships for follow-up. We want to connect them to a face, not just a place. For example, if they are a widow, a single mom, or a young adult, we want to make sure we get them connected to some great leaders in those areas who will continue to help them connect.

Serve Team 201

- Second Sunday of the month
- Following 11 a.m. service
- Taught by connections/serve team leader
- One hour and thirty minutes
- Teaching/assessment/tour
- Childcare provided
- Box lunch/water on table
- Round tables of 6 to 8
- Host/connector at each table

We call it the Serve Team, others call it the Dream Team, V-Team, Volunteers, etc. This is the awesome hands and feet expression of Jesus' church, empowered by spiritual gifts, conveying God's love by serving our church and community. It's the Church, the Body of Christ, in all of its gifting (see 1 Corinthians 12), connected and commissioned into action.

Serving is vital to one's connection in the church. As people serve together, they grow in relationship together. Relationships are the byproduct of a shared purpose. Everyone loves the experience of being on a winning team with a common vision. That's what using our gifts in the church should feel like. The 201 class is simply the on-ramp to bring this sense of purpose to people's lives so they can live this life of transcendence. It's what Jesus calls true greatness: serving others.

This Serve Team 201 class is awesome. It's a combination of inspirational teaching, self-discovery, and practical demonstration—all helping people connect by activating their spiritual gifts in the Body. Our goal coming out of this class is to get someone in a sweet spot on our Serve Team, connected to others, and using their gifts.

We start by casting a clear vision that we are an "everyone church." Everyone has a gift—the church needs their gift and their gift needs the church. Through a simple spiritual gift inventory and teaching on gifts, we help people discover the unique contribution they bring that makes us better as a church. We stay away from letting the specificity of the gift limit one's options to serve but instead focus on bringing their gift to a variety of opportunities.

> As people serve together, they grow in relationship together.

Following the teaching time, we present an array of opportunities for them to put their gifts to use on the Serve Team. While there are several unique opportunities, we start by encouraging them to choose from one of seven key areas: worship, children, students, first impressions, production, Small Groups, and local missions.

There are going to be people who have unique giftings or previous serving experience, but the majority of people want to know what we think they should do. They want to go where they are needed and can make a difference. Even if your church has many diverse serving opportunities, I think it's best to point people to fewer options to ensure a quicker and better on-boarding experience.

The table host is there to help work through the paperwork and work through the options to help them find something they are excited about. The host is so valuable at this time because people don't know what they don't know. The host can bring real clarity and direction.

Tour

After choosing one of the big seven Serve Team areas, we dismiss them to tour that area. Everyone gets up and heads out to clearly marked meeting points. A team leader meets them and begins to vision cast for the area and share the impact they can make. They walk them through the space they will be serving in, while telling stories of changed lives.

Obviously, this tour helps individuals become comfortable with the space, but the key is really comfort and confidence in the leader. Getting to meet face to face with the person who will help a volunteer on-board is a big difference maker. Follow-up without a face usually fails. But now they know exactly who the person calling, texting, and scheduling is, and this results in a better experience for everyone.

Follow-Up

Follow-up is an art. When it comes to volunteer follow-up, it's another level. People are busy and slow to add extra commitments to their calendars. This just means that you have to stay committed to it and keep the bigger vision in front of you. You are going to have to be patient and work with people and their schedules while pushing toward a commitment. As I said, it's another level.

It may take a few calls or emails before someone gets back to you. They have a lot going on, so the first one got lost, the second one made them feel bad for not responding to the first, and the third is a chance for redemption. I'll even respond to a solicitor on the third try, because I realize they're really serious about their product and serious about me.

When someone selects an area of service, the particular team leader is responsible for them winning in that area or helping them find another team. This means they may need to keep them on their radar for a month or so until they start actively serving. The leader makes sure they are followed up with, communicated clearly to, trained adequately, and appropriately placed.

> Everyone has a gift—the church needs their gift and their gift needs the church.

I don't want this to sound too heavy, but there really is no excuse for poor volunteer follow-up. The solution to every problem is more leaders, more great volunteers. No one should ever be too busy to follow up with new volunteers. On occasion I have heard someone say something to the tune of "I am still waiting to hear back" or "No one has followed up with me." That is like nails on a chalkboard. Take a minute to feel the jitters.

People are nervous to serve and communication is critical. What to wear and where to stand—seems obvious but it's not. We need to work hard to put together clear on-boarding communication. Anticipate their questions, give them helpful information, and you'll demonstrate your desire to help them succeed. You're helping them help you and a lot of other people.

Remember, serving is not casual to them like it may become to us. I remember recruiting a very successful business owner to be a door greeter. I was astounded by their questions and nervousness. "Do I stand on the right or the left? Do I say hello, hi, or good morning? When do I greet them? When they make eye contact or when they get to the door? Do I shake their hands, high five, fist bump, or nothing?"

It really reminded me of the seriousness of which our members approach serving. They are serving in the house of God and they feel the weight of it. You can open doors all day long for people anywhere else and not feel it, but when you are a greeter opening the doors to a church, you feel the weight of it. Our volunteers know the significance of coming through those doors and how it can change someone's entire life and eternity.

Leader Placement

I know this is a book on connection, not serving, but how well we handle the volunteer on-boarding determines how connected they stay. I want to say something that you will either get or you won't. Here it is: When placing people on teams, it's not just about what they are doing but who they are doing it with. Like the magnets on the front cover, they have to click.

This is highly intuitive, but certain people will follow some and not others. And they'll flow with some but not flow with others. It usually boils down to leadership gifting. It is hard to connect a higher-capacity leader on a lower-capacity leader's team. This is why we must constantly raise the leadership level of our teams by growing and recruiting higher-capacity leaders. And that keeps us personally needing to grow.

Higher-capacity leaders will raise the level of your teams, but they will also require more energy and shaping. Followers ask questions; leaders question you. Leading a leader looks more like Jesus leading Peter. He tried to question Jesus and command Him. But Jesus was secure. Jesus saw the potential in Peter, so He gave him time to work through his process. Jesus knew Peter could lead the other disciples once He was gone.

Values 301

- Sunday or Monday evenings
- Seven weeks long
- Taught by multiple teachers/pastors
- Childcare provided
- 30-minute teaching and 45-minute Small Group

As we work down the funnel, the final step in our Growth Track is a class we call Values 301. Different from the first two steps (101 and 201), this class is *seven weeks* long and meets on Sunday or Monday evenings for approximately 30 minutes of teaching and 45 minutes of Small Group. The commitment level goes up significantly, and as you would expect, we have to work much harder to help people prioritize this step.

The reason we opted for a multi-week process for this final Growth Track step came down to a values decision for us. We were willing to risk a slight decrease in participation if we could see a higher degree of impartation. Our hope is that participants don't just learn our values but begin to embody them. We wanted people to not just know we value connection to a spiritual family but also that we are working to help them experience it.

Imparting Our Values

We call this third step Values 301 because the goal is imparting our values. For our values to go from aspirational to actual we need to make sure those becoming part of Milestone Church value what we value. And that means not just knowing what we value as a church but also learning how to live those values out.

I'll share what we teach, but I am careful to not recommend anyone simply adopt our teaching topics. I think it is important that each church teaches what is most important or relevant to their context.

That being said, our seven-week class is broken down into five weeks where we discuss our core values (Bible, Mission, Spiritual Family, Development, and Generosity) and two weeks where we cover important teachings on salvation and baptism, and the Holy Spirit. Each week is an important combination of teaching and Small Group discussion. Not only is the content heard but also there is a place to process it.

Leaders Make the Difference

Finally, the success of our Values 301 class comes down to two things. First, as I already mentioned the teaching is an impartation, not just information; and second, the Small Group leaders are some of the best. Since we just talked through the teaching, I want to spend a minute on the impact of the Small Group leader.

With only a seven-week class, our Small Group leaders need to be secure and relationally intentional because there is a small window for connection. In the seven weeks, the leader is trying to learn the personal testimony of each individual in their group, connect them to each other, determine individual next steps, and finally nominate a leader from the bunch who will keep the group going.

After a couple rounds of leading, it is amazing how confident leaders become and how they get more and more purposeful with the pace. They learn the natural rhythms of folks opening up and the investment it takes outside of the group time to communicate and keep people synced up.

The goal at the end of the seven weeks is for the Small Group leader to have identified someone in the group who can continue to lead the group forward. The group could continue meeting in someone's home or at a coffee shop. This takes the intentional effort of the Values 301 leader going into it, knowing how they are going to transition the group at the close of the seven weeks.

Boats on the Dock

It's important to get the right people with the right captain in the right boat. That's the best metaphor I have to help people understand the key to relationships that click in the Values 301 class. Then it's simply a matter of launching ongoing Small Groups out of the seven-week class. When you have a bunch of new people looking for new friends on the dock, it's the best time to get them in some new boats.

Before we launch a class, we first select the highest caliber leaders, as mentioned in the previous section. Second, we go through every class registrant by name/family and then help group them with who we think they will best connect with. We look at pictures, membership forms, kids' ages, neighborhoods, schools, Facebook, etc., to find as many compatibility factors as possible. It's literally a Spirit-led matchmaking of relationships.

And we do pray to be Spirit-led in this, because we know how big of a deal these connections will be. Good connection equals a positive experience, potential lifelong friendships, and future spiritual support for one another. Bad connection equals a bad experience, lack of relationships, and a sense of disconnected-ness in our church. The positive or negative experience then dictates how someone speaks of the class and of the church going forward. All that to say, there is a lot at stake in these groupings. Don't get me wrong. I know God's sovereign, and we can't control people or their relationships, but I do think we should do our very best to steward people.

We group these people together and then help them board their boat (Small Group) where they will stay tied up to the dock for the next seven weeks of the class. At the end of the seven weeks, after hearing the values, growing together spiritually, and growing relationally, something great happens. The captain will designate a new captain, point to a new destination, get off the boat, and launch it out into the ocean of Small Groups. Now a new group, with new leadership, meeting off-site will continue on.

About half the time it happens just like described. Other times, the groups multiply and continue. Or if it was a couple's group, they launch out as two separate men's and women's groups. Sometimes the captain helps them just find other boats to get in, but the goal is that everybody still has a Small Group plan going forward.

I am giving you some great detail, but to be clear, I am not suggesting that anyone should do it exactly how we do it. Do the process that's best for the people, not people for the process. I think you should do what's best for your specific church context and to serve the amazing people coming to your church. Whatever it is, just make sure it's clear and everybody is on board.

Small Group Handoff

If the Growth Track is the process to help people find connection, Small Groups are the place to keep them connected. Small Groups are the Growth Track handoff. Connections are sustained through friendship cultivated over time in Small Groups. It may be a Small Group or Sunday school class, but the key is providing an environment small enough that relationships are developed, needs are met, prayers are prayed, and life is done—together.

My favorite scenario is a group of random people who start meeting together as a Small Group and eventually end up on vacation together as friends. Or young couples who start meeting together and begin having their first kids around the same time. It simply started with a shared meeting that became shared memories and shared lives.

It's in a Small Group that spiritual growth sinks its roots. We test the quality of our spiritual fruit when we walk in close relationships with others. We don't even know we are selfish until we practice serving and deferring to one another. We get to practice repentance and forgiveness as we offend one another but pursue unity and reconciliation. It's in Small Groups that we study the Bible but also get to live out what it says.

This sense of spiritual family doesn't happen overnight, but it does happen over time. Eventually they have what everyone wants: a group of friends who know them, care about them, and share the ups and downs of life with them. Everyone wants to know someone is there to pray for them and help them in their moment of crisis; this someone is often their Small Group. I've seen many people leave churches for various reasons, but they don't quickly leave their Small Group. Those connections are too vital.

Key Takeaways

- A Growth Track is a series of classes with intentional teaching and connection to facilitate spiritual growth and engagement.
- From the top of the organization and throughout, everyone needs to believe the Growth Track is the lifeblood of the church, not simply a side ministry in the church.
- A Growth Track tells people coming to your church that you have a plan for their growth and connection.
- Church members should be excited to refer people to the Growth Track. If not, we need to work on some things and make it better.
- As people serve together, they grow in relationships together.
- Everyone has a gift—the church needs their gift and their gift needs the church.
- When placing people on teams, it's not just about what they are doing but also about who they are doing it with.
- We wanted people to not just know we value connection to a spiritual family but also to help them experience that in the Growth Track process.

Reflection Questions

1. Does your church have a clear Growth Track?
2. Are your church staff and key leaders excited about your Growth Track process?
3. Does your current Growth Track process produce the spiritual engagement and connection steps you are looking for?

15

TRACK THE GROWTH
(THE PEOPLE BOARD)

*Be shepherds of God's flock that is under your
care, watching over them—not because you
must, but because you are willing, as God
wants you to be; not pursuing dishonest gain,
but eager to serve.*

1 PETER 5:2, NIV

It's the secret sauce, the winning play, the card up our sleeve—
it's the People Board. It's what every church pastor/lead-
er wants to see when they visit Milestone. People fly in from
around the country just to see our board of amazing people.
But as you can imagine, it's more than a board; it's a representation of Milestone's relentless heart of connection and value
for people.

What better way to keep watch over the flock that is under our
care than to literally keep watch over them. From someone's first
step of engagement in the Growth Track, we take their picture
and keep watch over them on the People Board. We remember

who they are and can see what step is in front of them. Our team prays over them and follows up to help them take their next step.

As we've grown, our board has become an entire wall in the office that allows us to track every person's step in our growth track and into Small Groups and serving. Starting with Discovery 101, we simply track their picture, moving them down the board, through steps of engagement (101, 201, 301, Small Group, and serving). At a glance we can see how we are doing at assimilation; and with some focus, we can see how any particular individual is doing.

Whenever I visit the People Board in our office, it makes me smile. It's moving to see the people God has brought our way to care for, disciple, and equip. I love celebrating the steps people are taking and I get burdened for those lagging behind. We are called to keep watch over the sheep, and this is the most practical way I have found to do that.

We keep their face in front of us for a year. That's twelve months of intentionally communicating with them, casting vision for opportunities, working through their busy schedules to help them take steps. It's not that after a year we stop serving them, but we transition to a more general approach.

The Origin of the People Board

When the church was smaller, we didn't need a People Board. We were killing it. We knew who was new and what steps they had taken. We also knew the leaders to connect them to and made sure to keep in touch with those not yet connected.

We started growing faster, and I remember losing track of people's names and faces. Up until that point, I could name most every family in our church, I could point out first-time guests, and I knew where almost everyone was serving. But with the growth we were experiencing, this all changed, and our team began to lose its connective edge.

Our follow-up process became a long report of names we'd pull from our database and work through like a checklist. Faceless cold calls and emails weren't producing the same engagement we previously had, and I was getting frustrated. I loved that we had the information, but there was no life, no personality, no connection. Something was missing—the face.

My leading thought was, *Let's put a face to every name and know the name of every face.* I wanted our teams to be able to connect not just names from reports but also the faces with the names. This enabled us to utilize some memory recall and connection equity that came with remembering who someone is. "Oh yeah, I remember talking to . . . They're friends with . . . Moved here from . . ."

> Let's put a face to every name and know the name of every face.

I wanted our team and key leaders to be able to picture the face they were praying for and help with next steps but also remember their names. I often go over to the People Board just to help refresh myself on names. I don't know any other way to do it than to scan the board of faces and do a name refresh. Our database allows us to search a face from a name, but this is the only way to find a name from a face. And as I said in a previous chapter, knowing names is knowing people, and it's the greatest communication of value.

My second thought with the People Board was, *Let's guarantee that nobody falls through the cracks.* I wanted to ensure that every person who attends our church could be known, connected, and pastored as they engaged in our Growth Track and Small Groups. What better way to ensure they do not fall through the cracks than to put their picture on the wall.

I know there are more technological ways to do things, but I have not yet come up with something that visually captures each individual's journey as well as seeing their picture on a wall and the step they are in. The only way someone could fall through the cracks is if they fall off the wall. This did happen once, and one of our little people was carried off on the bottom of someone's shoe, but we recovered them.

Here's the backstory of the People Board. As you may have experienced, all of our amazing church members were getting stuck in the computer. Connection cards would come in, membership forms would come in, and they'd get entered into the computer. Even as they went into the computer, I was so slow to throw out the card, or the form, because even just the handwriting brought some personality to it.

I started asking questions of how to solve this. Surely someone has faced this dilemma. As I was asking around, a representative of our church management software recommended adding people's pictures to their profile in the database. The idea surfaced that we could take pictures of every person who attends our Discovery 101 (first-step Growth Track class) and add a picture to their profile.

I am embarrassed to say my first reaction was, "No way! These people haven't even decided if they want to join. Some aren't even Christians yet. We can't run them off by taking their picture!" After a little calming and convincing from our team, I acquiesced to experiment with the idea.

At the next Discovery 101 we rolled it out and I was ready for the uproar, people storming out, protesting even. None of that happened. People actually enjoyed it. In the ten-plus years we've done it, maybe a handful have politely declined. What we have gotten is thousands of pictures of the awesome Milestone people in our system, allowing us to serve them at the next level.

Joy-Ann, our amazing Growth Track Director, has been the brains behind developing this process into what it is today. It works because she cares so deeply for each individual and constantly tweaks our process to really pray for and take care of each person who starts the Growth Track. Plus, she's British, so whenever she talks about the People Board process, it just sounds extra awesome!

The whole church benefits from this intentionality. Our People Board and picture-capture process serves the entire team. What

I mean is, because we do this, whenever someone searches for a name in the database, that person's picture comes up. Think about how helpful that is for connecting, recruiting, and training.

> Let's guarantee that nobody falls through the cracks.

If, for example, you are trying to remember who John Smith is, it is as simple as putting his name in the database and there he is. Volunteer leaders can be given printouts to help them remember their team members, serve them more effectively, and pray for them more specifically. I want all of our volunteer leaders to have a printout of pictures so they can pray for their team members by name and face.

How We Do It

We capture individuals' pictures at our first step in the Growth Track, the Discovery 101 class. We simply make it part of the check-in process. They walk up and get their name tag. (If pre-registered, we already have it printed for them.) Next, they take a few more steps to an area with adequate lighting and a solid background where we can take their picture. "Smile!"

Our volunteer team uses an iPad or phone to take pictures, nothing fancy. The key is to make sure to get a good framed shot of the individual and include the name tag. This is a very helpful key to keep the names and the faces in sync. Trust me, we learned this the hard way.

After we capture their pictures, the next step is to upload them to our church management database. Most church databases have this capability, or you may be able to figure out an even better way to catalogue the pictures. So, following their attendance in our Discovery 101 class, we now have great contact information, personal information, and even a picture that we can add to their profile.

After all the necessary info gets inputted, we get them back out of the computer. We print out everyone's picture on little 1" x 1½" rectangles and start the whole class at the top of the board. Our process has evolved and we now laminate the pictures and affix tiny magnets behind each, allowing us to move them with ease on our magnetic boards.

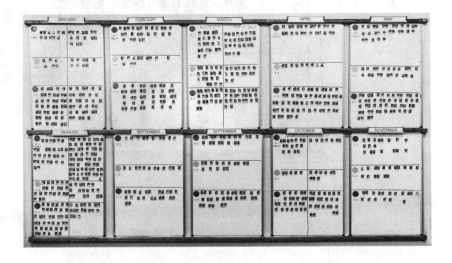

As I said, we track each adult individual for one year on the board. We keep them categorized by the month they started the Growth Track, such as "February 2019." Each month has three sections from top to bottom: 101, 201, 301—our three Growth Track steps. We move them down to each section as they attend/complete each step. Along with moving them down, we have other stickers we use to let us know if they are in a Small Group or have an active serving assignment.

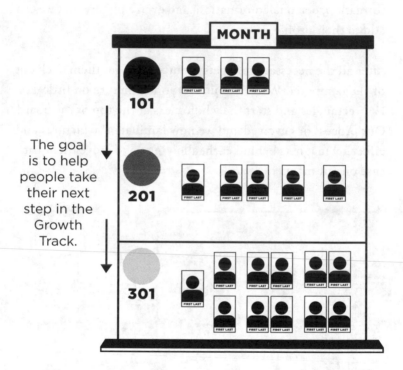

At our central campus, we currently have approximately 1,300 faces on our board, divided up by the month they started the Growth Track—so approximately 100 per month. It's a lot, but it still works like it did 10 years ago.

All that to say, I think we've tested its ability to serve people from small scale to large scale. It doesn't matter the scale; one picture is one person we get to connect spiritually and relationally in our church and equip them for their ministry. And we need to serve a bunch of individuals just like they're the only one.

You Can Do It!

Wherever you are, you can start now to capture pictures and serve people at another level by seeing names and faces. Even if you do not adopt the People Board process, I encourage you to at least incorporate a picture with their profile to better remember who they are and keep their face in front of you. It's not too late to start. Think about it: the people who need this most are those newest or not yet in your church. So your implementation of this process will be right on time for them.

Start with who God is sending. Even if it's just one person this month, how intentional can we be with the one? Put their picture on the board so the whole staff can pray for them, know their name, know their face, and believe great things for them. I think that's what Jesus would be thinking.

We started the chapter with Peter's words to the church. But it all started with Jesus' words to Peter. Jesus was serious about loving people well. When we go to the next level to love people well, we are loving Jesus well.

> *The third time he said to him, "Simon son of John,*
> *do you love me?" Peter was hurt because Jesus*

asked him the third time, "Do you love me?" He said, "Lord, you know all things; you know that I love you." Jesus said, "Feed my sheep."

JOHN 21:17, NIV

Key Takeaways

- Be shepherds of God's flock that is under your care, watching over them (see 1 Peter 5:2).
- The best way to keep watch over people is to actually keep watch over them with the help of a People Board.
- From someone's first step of engagement in the Growth Track, we take their picture, put it on the People Board, and help them keep taking steps in the Growth Track.
- The goal is to put a face to every name and know the name of every face.
- We keep each person's picture up on the People Board for one year as we prayerfully help them make connections, complete the Growth Track, and find a Small Group.
- It's more than just a board of pictures; it's a representation of Milestone Church's relentless heart of connection and value for people.
- This effort is a way to help ensure that nobody falls through the cracks.

Reflection Questions

1. Do you already have a process in place to capture people's pictures?
2. How much easier would follow-up be when you know the name/face of the person you are contacting?
3. Would you consider something like a People Board for your church?

CONCLUSION

There is nothing I want more than to see the time and energy I put into this book enlarge your life personally, impact your church, and see more people connected to the Body of Christ. I pray for doors of opportunity to open for you as you open doors for others. I pray for people to flood through the doors of your church as teams of leaders are equipped to connect them and lead them to a relationship with Jesus Christ. And I pray God gives you wisdom to build on the teachings of this book and make them even greater for your church.

Your church, leadership, culture, and even vision are unique. Please entertain the ideas I have presented but then filter them through what is best for you. Before implementation of processes, first properly submit them to leadership to make sure there is unity. What is best for my church may not be what is best for yours. Unity is what God blesses, even before good ideas (see Psalm 133).

In conclusion, I would just say thank-you. We may not know each other, but if you picked up this book and got as far as the conclusion, then we have a bond even greater than the words we've shared on these pages. We share a belief that the local church, even with her flaws, is beautiful. We believe that relationships are messy but awesome and matter deeply to what God is doing.

And finally, we care for the outsider, the disconnected, and the one who Jesus and all of heaven is always thinking about.

If I can help you further, please don't hesitate to contact me. Also, I would love to learn from you, as well as hear your thoughts on the book. I do hope our paths cross as we serve together connecting the world to Jesus.

I look forward to connecting with you!

Steve
steve.chesnut@milestonechurch.com
Twitter: @SteveChesnut
Instagram: chesnut.steve

APPENDIX

VALUES 301 OVERVIEW

Week 1: Spiritual Family

"God sets the lonely in families." That's what the Bible says in Psalm 68:6. We want people to understand their church engagement is not casual. Church engagement is not a practical choice or a consumeristic experience but a revelation of where and to whom God is joining them. When someone understands God has "set" them, it changes the way they give to and receive from the family.

The Small Group relationships they are building are a starting point for practicing spiritual family. They will have an opportunity to pray for one another, use their gift to build up one another, and opportunities to serve one another. Along the way it may really get tested as they walk through offense and sacrifice for one another, which is the true test of family.

Week 2: Salvation and Water Baptism

Even though we have already presented the gospel in Discovery 101, we still think it is important to share it again in our Values

301 class. For whatever reason, people are a process and we find that this is the moment many are ready to take that step of faith or take a step closer. They also have a Small Group now and the opportunity to dialogue about their questions.

The second part of the teaching is water baptism. We are a baptism-by-immersion church and believe it is one's next step after committing their life to Christ. Some people have received Jesus but never been baptized, and we point them to their next step. Others have been baptized as infants, or before their faith became their own, and we help them understand believer's baptism. That is, you first personally believe in the Lord Jesus for salvation and then you are water baptized.

Week 3: Missional Living

One of our core values is mission. That is defined as our partnership with Jesus in His mission known as the Great Commission. This is a together mission with Jesus to make disciples both near and far. The same way people get pumped up to go far on a mission trip to share Jesus, we want them just as pumped to go to their workplaces, classrooms, and neighborhoods to share Jesus and invite people to church.

A main focus is a concept we call missional living. This is the idea that evangelism is not something we turn on or off but a way we live our lives: constantly active, open, and looking for where God is moving around us and moving us to make Him known. This could be purposeful kindness, sharing the gospel, or inviting someone to church.

Week 4: The Bible

Another core value we unpack is our value for the Bible. We teach and believe that it is the holy, inspired, infallible Word of God. If the Bible says it, that settles it. Our opinions matter on some things but not on matters the Bible has already spoken to.

The Bible is the living and active Word of God (see Hebrews 4:12), and when it is acted on, it becomes alive in us. We teach that we don't pick and choose what we like out of the Bible, but we predetermine to obey what it says—because it's not simply a book we read, but it reads us. We also encourage practical memorization and confession of God's Word as part of our daily lives.

Week 5: The Holy Spirit

We spend a week on the Holy Spirit because we have found there to be much curiosity and confusion in our specific church context. When it comes to the teaching on the Holy Spirit, there are two sections. The first section is the person of the Holy Spirit and the second is more of the work of the Holy Spirit.

It is important to clearly define what you believe, because what's not defined can create division. People come from all different backgrounds. I am shocked by the extremes when it comes to teachings on the person and work of the Holy Spirit. I am not going to get into what we teach, or pretend we have perfected it. But I would encourage your church to teach what you believe to bring new believers and church transfers to a place of unity.

Week 6: Generosity

This is another core value we celebrate and don't hide from. Generosity brings life to people, environments, even churches. It's not just being generous with our money but also generous with our relational energy, abilities, and consideration of others. When we are generous and give of ourselves, we receive so much more.

We also teach on the biblical principles of financial giving in this section. We are upfront on our belief in the tithe as the starting point of stewardship. We don't limit it there but also encourage Spirit-led giving, first-fruit giving, and special sacrificial offerings in response to a great need.

Week 7: Development

Our final core value is development. We present this as a commitment of the church to create opportunities for individuals to continue to personally develop—also as a challenge for them to begin to assist in the development of others.

There are unlimited next steps of development in the local church. Individuals can develop their spiritual leadership by leading teams, Small Groups, Sunday school classes, internships, personal discipleship, etc. Individuals can be developed in their marriage, parenting, and even as a Christian businessperson.

We also have a high expectation we communicate: that they will begin to develop others (commonly known as discipleship).

Discipleship is simply disciples making disciples who make disciples. Call it development, coaching, or mentoring—it's helping someone else take next steps.

DEVELOPMENT GROUPS

Background

Several years back, we looked around our church and found a lot of men who were good at getting married, starting families, and building careers—but no one was building them. No one was helping them stay married, be the spiritual leader of the home, or find fulfillment in their career. We thought men wanted a pancake breakfast, but what they really wanted was to be challenged with a purpose and connected with other men.

Pastor Jeff started leading men's development groups to help men win in the areas of life that matter most. Now, many years later, *The Way to Win* book directly addresses the recurring themes he found to be most helpful in building the lives of leaders who have become the core spiritual leaders of our church.

The Development Group concept and *The Way to Win* resource were designed to make men rich where they're poor by helping them win in their spiritual life, character, relationships, and legacy. Driven men know how to educate themselves and go after what they want, but it takes other men to help them become a man of God and choose to go after what matters most.

Group Experience

The best groups are built when a capable leader selects individuals of a similar drive who commit to the journey together. Most common groupings are one leader, 10 men, meeting weekly before work, for approximately 10 months. The journey often starts with a group of guarded strangers but ends with a band of brothers building the Kingdom together.

- Weekly one-hour group
- Read one chapter of *The Way to Win* each week
- Cover chapter discussion questions
- Approximately 40 weeks long (10 months)

Content

After years of compiling the best biblical teachings and practical resources to help men grow, we compiled them into one dedicated resource, *The Way to Win* book. Each of the 38 concise and direct chapters include discussion questions to make reading and application very attainable.

Section 1: The Winning Lifestyle – Personal Development
Section 2: The Winning Fundamentals – Spiritual Foundations
Section 3: The Winning Playbook – Character Development
Section 4: The Winning Culture – Values
Section 5: The Winning Strategy – Discipleship

To learn more, please visit resources.milestonechurch.com.

CONNECTION CARD

FRONT

CONNECTION CARD

Scan QR code for digital card option

☐ 1st Time Guest   ☐ Regular Attender/Member

☐ 2nd / 3rd Time Guest   ☐ Update My Info

Date:_____

SAT	SUN
☐ 5:00pm ☐ 6:30pm	☐ 9:15am ☐ 11:00am ☐ 12:30pm

(Please print)

Name: _____

Spouse (if applicable): _____

Address:_____

_____

City:_____ State: _____ Zip: _____

Contact #: (_____)_____ ☐ H ☐ C ☐ W

Email:_____

DOB:____/____/_____ Spouse:____/____/_____

HOW DID YOU HEAR ABOUT US?

(Name of person who invited you, postcard, internet search, etc.)

_____

_____

_____

Place this card in one of our giving boxes
as you exit the Worship Center.

BACK

SIGN ME UP FOR THE NEXT....

☐ Discovery 101   ☐ Values 301
☐ Serve Team 201

I'M INTERESTED IN...

☐ Serving
☐ Joining a Small Group
☐ Local/Global Outreach

MY DECISION...

☐ I prayed today to receive Jesus
☐ I prayed to renew my commitment to Jesus
☐ I want to be water baptized

PRAYER REQUEST

We value praying for one another. Please let us know
how can we pray for you or offer pastoral care.

_____

_____

_____

_____

_____

_____

_____

_____

Place this card in one of our giving boxes
as you exit the Worship Center.

MILESTONE CHURCH
Reaching People. Building Lives.

Please e-mail any comments or suggestions to info@milestonechurch.com

FRONT

BACK

ACKNOWLEDGMENTS

This would not have been possible without the incredible Milestone team that has lived out this book on a weekly basis and helped bring it all together.

To Jed Walker and Mel Baggett, who reviewed, edited, and contributed to the formation of this book. It would not have been possible without you.

Thank you, Haley Gauthier and Blake Campbell, for the amazing art and layout; as well as Marie Prestwood and Tasha Ray, for your hard work bringing this book to print.

To my executive assistant, Alyssa Zetsche, who keeps things moving so well, and to ministry resident Hannah Milner, for jumping in to finish out the project. And to our Growth Track Director, Joy-Ann Curd, who stewards people so brilliantly, and super-connector Ty Spinella, our Executive Director of Connections.

To Pat Brown, for overseeing all things involving our Serve Team and First Impressions with a tremendous team: Kalan Richards, Eddie Guerra, and Liz Wagner.

I would also like to honor some local church-connections leaders I respect very much. Thank you for being early readers of the manuscript and providing me valuable input to help guide the formation of the book: Kyle Jackson, Cary Robinson, Ron Stegall, Danny Franks, Jeff Pelletier, and Caleb Fauber.

And finally, where it all began, my loving parents, who model a love for God and a love for people so well.

ENDNOTES

1   Ben Sasse, *Them* (New York: St. Martin's Press, 2018), p. 29.

2   Maya Angelou, https://www.goodreads.com/quotes/5934-i-ve-learned-that-people-will-forget-what-you-said-people.

3   Horste Schulze, *Excellence Wins* (Grand Rapids, MI: Zondervan, 2019), pp. 38-39.

4   See Matthew 4:19-22.

5   See Matthew 14:13-21.

6   See John 18:10.

7   Michael J. Gelb, *The Art of Connection* (Novato, CA: New World Library, 2017), p. 23.

8   Ralph Waldo Emerson, https://www.forbes.com/quotes/7810/.

9   Schulze, *Excellence Wins*, p. 47.

10 Simon Sinek, "The Power of Kindness," https://youtu.be/8afO6jkod_4.

11 Malcolm Gladwell, *The Tipping Point* (New York: Hachette Book Group, 2002), p. 37.

12 Ed Stetzer and Thom Ranier, *Transformational Church* (Nashville, TN: B&H Publishing, 2010), p. 206.

13 Edward T. Hall, *The Hidden Dimension* (New York: Random House, 1966), n.p.

14 Dr. Martin Luther King Jr., "Drum Major Instinct" Sermon at Ebenezer Baptist Church, 1968, https://kinginstitute.stanford.edu/king-papers/publications/knock-midnight-inspiration-great-sermons-reverend-martin-luther-king-jr-8.

15 Danny Franks, *People Are the Mission* (Grand Rapids, MI: Zondervan, 2018), p. 94.

VISIT US ONLINE

MILESTONECHURCH.COM

CONNECT WITH MILESTONE CHURCH
@MILESTONECHURCH

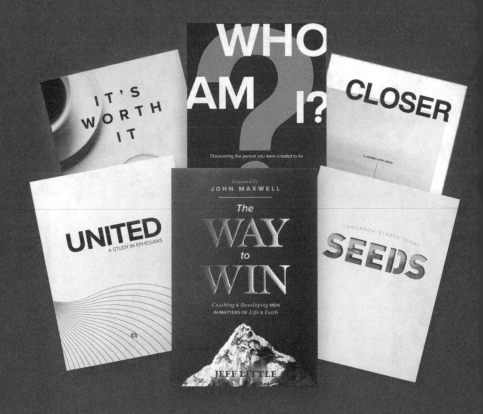